IT'S
COMPLICATED

IT'S COMPLICATED

COLLECTED CONFESSIONS OF MESSY MODERN LOVE

PHILIPPA FOUND

PAVILION

Pavilion
An imprint of HarperCollins*Publishers* Ltd
1 London Bridge Street
London SE1 9GF

www.harpercollins.co.uk

HarperCollins*Publishers*
Macken House
39/40 Mayor Street Upper
Dublin 1
D01 C9W8
Ireland

10 9 8 7 6 5 4 3 2

First published in Great Britain by
Pavilion, an imprint of
HarperCollins*Publishers* Ltd 2025

Copyright © Philippa Found 2025

Philippa Found asserts the moral right
to be identified as the author of this
work. A catalogue record for this book
is available from the British Library.

ISBN 978-0-00-865260-9

Printed and bound in London, UK
by CPI

Publishing Director: Laura Russell
Commissioning Editor: Ellen Simmons
Design Manager: Alice Kennedy-Owen
Copyeditor: Corinne Colvin
Proofreader: Kathy Woolley
Production Controller: Emma Hatlen

This book contains FSC™ certified paper and other controlled
sources to ensure responsible forest management.

For more information visit: www.harpercollins.co.uk/green

For my best friend, Lucie –
I wish you were here.

For Tigs and Romy.

And for anyone who ever thought they were
the only one to feel that way: you're not.

CONTENTS

SWIPE RIGHT

SINGLE

HOOKING UP

DATING

IT'S COMPLICATED

FRIENDS & FAMILY

IN A RELATIONSHIP

SWIPE RIGHT

(INTRODUCTION)

If you've ever found yourself alone at 2 a.m. checking
your ex's social media – or their new partner's LinkedIn
(because it's the only social profile you can access) – or
if you've been having sex with your partner knowing
they're making love and you're making plans to leave –
or if you can't stop thinking about the one who broke
your heart a decade ago – or if everyone thinks you're the
perfect couple but you haven't had sex for years – or if
you're swiping to fill a void – or if you know you'll still
drop everything for them even though you know you're
just an option for them – then you've probably felt a
smarting of shame. That burning, poisonous, suffocating
feeling that there is something deeply, uniquely wrong
with you; with your desires, or your lack of desires,
or your inability to move on – your inability to be the
person that you think you *should* be. But let me tell
you something radical: your darkest secrets, your most
repulsively shameful thoughts, feelings and behaviours:
you're not alone in them. They're normal.

I know this because on 7th May 2020, in the
depths of global lockdown, I created a website –
lockdownlovestories.com – which allowed people to
anonymously submit their true stories of how lockdown
had affected their relationships. I'd believed the shift in

relationships would be monumental – couples, friends and families forced to suddenly separate or quarantine together for an unknown amount of time; single people living without touch – the reality of our relationships that we'd previously been able to distract ourselves from, now confronting us, and amplified. I wanted to tell that story; to create a time capsule of a moment in history, a collective portrait of love in extreme circumstances. But, more than this, I wanted to alleviate the subsidiary shame of all the heartbreak, loss, and loneliness people might experience, and to counter the insidious damage of all the filtered, curated edits of social media's life highlights and #couplegoals by creating a platform for sharing something a little more real. I wanted to show others that they weren't the only ones going through it.

As an artist and writer, my practice explores desire, shame, and millennial miscommunications and misinterpretations. It is rooted in the belief that autobiography and storytelling can be used as a radical act to counter the oppression of shame, which can silence our messy, complex, but actually completely normal experiences.

To counter shame you need two things: a safe space to express how you're feeling, and you also need to be able to see that your experiences are not unique. There needs to be an acceptance that your experience is universal; that others are feeling the same way you are. You need to know that what you're feeling is not weird or wrong; that *you* are not, fundamentally, weird or wrong.

That is what shame is: the belief that there is something uniquely wrong with you.

Shame grows in silence. If met with the words, 'me too', shame diminishes. Sharing helps; recognition helps more.

My website allowed anyone to submit their story anonymously, with no trace of where it had come from. Like a Catholic confession, where there's no need to show your face. Or therapy, without the financial barrier. It was somewhere you were able to access other people's therapy sessions too, because every story submitted was published anonymously on the website.

More than 1,500 stories were shared on the site, and just over 250 of those stories are brought together here, in *It's Complicated*.

These are real, everyday people's unedited, raw, intimate, true stories of love and relationships. Many are testimony to the endurance of human connection even in the most disconnected of circumstances. What is most apparent is that *all* these stories tell us *how it feels* to love – in all its complex, sticky messiness. How it feels to fall in love, to fall out of love, to still wonder 'why?' many years after a break-up, to pretend to be totally cool over text while you're crying in the back of the Uber, to negate your needs because you're holding out hope. These stories give honest and poignant accounts of how it really feels to be single, to date, to be in a relationship, to break up, and they reveal all the contradictions of every relationship state. We are exposed to the most desirable side of life on social media, but these stories dare to cover the full spectrum – showing the multifaceted, complicated reality of our emotional experiences, as well as the harder, darker things that we hadn't previously been honest about. The reason the stories are so compelling is because they are so relatable. Experiences we thought might be wholly personal were revealed to be shared. There is something very reassuring in that.

We all love love stories, but there is a particular power in true stories from ordinary people like us. The happy stories give hope – *if it happened to them, it could happen to me* – and the darker stories give reassurance – *it's not just me*. Through recognition of shared experience and the emotions underpinning these experiences, storytelling has the unique capacity to incite empathy that can unite us in times of polarity, disconnect and crisis by reminding us of our shared humanity.

Yet for too long the same stories have been told, and others unheard. Gathering submissions through guerrilla advertising – chalking the lockdown love stories website URL in parks (firstly alone on my daily lockdown walks, and then across the country thanks to a team of volunteers) and exhibiting the stories on the public transport network and on the high street – was done with an activist intent of reaching a wide, diverse public; to collect stories from voices not necessarily traditionally represented in arts or literature. Through the internet, another democratic space, word of the project spread across the world. The resulting collection of stories comes from teenagers to octogenarians, from London to Melbourne. The anonymity of the submission process removed another potential barrier to representation, allowing people to share candidly without inhibition, and invite the reader to move away from heteronormative readings and not assume the gender of the writer. Instead, the stories tell us about love in all forms, at all ages: falling in love in your twenties, dating in your fifties, fifty-year affairs in your seventies, reconnecting with childhood love in your eighties. They tell of being happily single, anxiously single, ecstatically coupled, ambivalently coupled – and everything in between. Their collective range is nuanced and vital to remind us that there is no 'normal' way to feel.

This is essential to dismantling shame. Internal shame is triggered when we judge ourselves to be failing in some way; not living up to what we perceive as expected, violating a social norm, not feeling the way we believe we are *supposed* to feel, or not being the type of person we believe we *should* be. So, when we share our true stories without inhibition or fear of judgment – revealing the dark as well as the light, the conflicted as well as the resolved – collectively we begin to expand our idea of normality, making it more inclusive, until we rupture the idea of 'normal' entirely, and in doing so begin to free ourselves from that shame of 'failing'.

It is also only through representation that we learn that our story matters. Whoever we are and whatever our experiences, our truths *are* powerful. Testimony to this, a year into the pandemic, my project was awarded the London Community Story Grant (part of the Greater London Authority's community-led recovery programme launched by the Mayor of London) to bring insights to City Hall to inform post-pandemic mental-health recovery policy: a legacy that shows the very real impact that speaking out loud can have, and how vital it is to share these accounts to try to bring about societal change.

It's Complicated brings together a selection of those 1,500 confessions, arranged by relationship status – Exes, Single, Hooking Up, Dating, It's Complicated, Friends & Family, In a Relationship, and Break-ups – to reveal how we really experience those relationship stages.

In *Exes* there are stories of being unable to move on: deep-diving social media; still thinking about an ex even after marrying and having two kids with someone else; finding out the one that got away just got engaged. There are stories of chance encounters and conscious reconnections; of having your heart broken by the same guy for the second time (twenty-six years later); as well as stories of finally blocking, deleting and moving on.

Single brings together stories of wild sex dreams and living without touch; approaching thirty never having been kissed; going for years without sex; to stories of not waiting for anyone else to build the life that you want for yourself. There are stories of deleting all your dating apps and redirecting that energy on yourself; how it feels when everyone thinks you're living your best life but you can't stop comparing yourself to your married friends; and stories of how it feels to want to find a partner in a culture of, at times, toxic positivity surrounding independence and self-love.

There are stories about casual sex, experimentation and sexual frustrations in *Hooking Up* – of sex in parks with strangers, Sundays at sex clubs, threesomes on video call, hooking up with couples, sex in long-distance relationships, and masturbation. Stories of moving beyond your comfort zone, adaptation, and the self-discovery that can come from the exploration of pleasure.

Dating explores the reality of the journey, from meeting someone (whether IRL or virtually) to getting into a relationship – or not – and navigating everything that comes in between: blue ticks, red flags, love bombing, ghosting, the alchemic rush of a new connection, feeling like you may have finally met The One. There are stories of dates that cancel when they're parked outside your house, requests for period sex, ghosting, the awkwardness of mismatched feelings, calling out flaky behaviour and demanding respect, and changing what you look for in a match and finding a new outcome.

The section *It's Complicated* includes stories of coming to terms with your sexuality twenty years into a marriage; navigating polyamory; falling in love with your best friend when you thought you were straight, years of mismatched timing aligning; and forty-three attempts at getting over someone. There are stories of those slippery situationships that defiantly, and often maddeningly, evade definition; the clusterfuck of being friends and maybe-but-not-definitely-more and falling in love when you – or they – are unavailable.

In *Friends & Family* there are love stories about ride-or-die friends who are there through everything, picking you up when you fall on your face in the supermarket post-break-up-drunk as well as the lesser spoken heartbreaks of friendships ending. There are stories of the formative, at times dysfunctional, dynamics in families, and the complex relationships between mothers and daughters at all ages. There are stories about the healing power of pets that are there for you, unconditionally and uncomplicatedly, and stories of the wild ride of motherhood: from the fierce longing to conceive, the pain of watching friends' growing bumps, the heartbreak of miscarriage, to the identity-shattering-heart-smashed-open claustrophobic love of new motherhood.

In a Relationship reveals the reality of being in a relationship beyond the cute announcement posts we see online: from the understated acts that are the cement of long-term relationships – morning cups of teas brought to bed, binge-watching box sets, wordless hand-held walks – to the shadow sides we don't often shout about: comparisons with exes, the struggle of trying to move past infidelity, discovering your partner has a drug problem. There are stories of growing together and growing apart, the shifts and synergies in long-term love, co-dependency, claustrophobia, the agony of lying next to a partner longing for them to hold you, and the throat-tightening paralysis of falling out of love but being afraid to leave.

Finally, there are stories of *Break-ups* and their aftermath. From accounts of bumping into an ex for the first time after a break-up, to a break-up call documented word for word. There are accounts of break-up grief that outlives houseplants, to break-ups that allow you to re-explore your sexuality. There are stories of moving on, and stories of not having moved on 365 days later, stories that articulate the acute pain of break-ups, the stodginess of wading through them, as well as the freedom and hope of new beginnings.

These are fierce, vulnerable stories that are by turns funny, sexy, heart-breaking and heart-warming – but above all, they are honest. They are stories that are so relatable that at times it felt as if someone had stolen my secrets and sent them to me. Stories that, at first, played out against the backdrop of a pandemic, but moved far beyond to reveal the intimate and often unspoken, inconvenient realities of love at all times. They are stories of our complexities, our messiness, our conflicting desires. Stories that tell us not who we *should* be, but who we *are*.

I hope that this book provides some balance to our internalised, idealised beliefs about relationships. I hope you find your story inside these pages, in someone else's words. And I hope that that alleviates the shame that you need not carry.

To every person who took their truth and brought it out of the darkness for others to better know they're not alone: Thank you.

EXES

If you've ever lost someone you truly loved, you've probably wondered *What if?*. What if that thing hadn't happened? What if I'd said that? What if we were together now? Do they still think of me? How are they really? What if I just messaged them?

Thinking of an ex can create a heady cocktail of nostalgia, melancholy and romanticising the past. We romanticise who we were, who we could have been and what our shared life could have looked like. Added to this, love doesn't really ever go away, and we don't want to be forgotten. We daydream, we think about getting in touch, we check their social media. Most of the time, we decide – whether for reasons of pride, realism, respect, fear, self-awareness – that it's best not to.

Our culture celebrates moving on, while simultaneously facilitating the temptation to look back through social media. It suggests that not looking back is a sign of success, proof of having graduated to better things; that self-love and sufficient self-worth mean deleting, blocking and believing you are better off without what has passed. However, the possibility of searching for traces of your ex (at least virtually) is always only a few clicks away. This can make moving on harder, but also means that not being able to move on becomes laced with a sense of failure and shame.

But we've all wondered, haven't we? What if you could re-encounter the intensity of your first love, with the benefit of all the wisdom gained since? Wouldn't that be the greatest? Wouldn't it end differently this time?

These are stories of missing people and of longing. Of the internalised shame of not being 'over it', of wondering how long it will take, of searching social media for their face, and of posting for only *their* reaction. These are stories of the desire to reconnect and of having to constantly, consciously stop yourself. There are stories of hearing from, or bumping into, exes and being pulled back in – or finally getting closure. These are stories of second chances, of new perspectives, of old patterns and forging new ones. There are stories of feeling stuck, of the liberation of no longer wanting something that you held in thrall, and of the empowerment of realising that sometimes the person you're trying to get back is not them, but a version of you.

These are stories of what happens when our past and present lives collide.

MY ONE LOVE

He is, and always has been, my one love. We were
together when we were sixteen, but eventually broke
up in our twenties after we grew up, and grew apart.
He used to take me for granted; I used to nag him.

A decade later, we had lost touch completely. A couple
of years ago I started to dream – vivid, realistic dreams –
about him. I would wake up devastated. I found myself
longing for that familiarity, that closeness that I hadn't
found again since.

One day, I was feeling lonelier than ever. I texted a
friend explaining how I kept thinking about him. I looked
up his Instagram, watching from afar at this exciting life
he was living without giving me a second thought. I felt
heartbroken.

The next day, completely out of the blue, he slid into
my DMs. Call it a rom-com or blame the algorithms from
the stalking... but we arranged to meet for coffee. It's
amazing how you can know a person inside and out but
they can still make you as nervous as hell to see them
again.

Turns out, he felt the same all this time too. It's like it
was meant to be. All signs pointing to destiny.

Oh – but he has a girlfriend.

So, I'm trying my hardest to keep my options open;
trying to be a good person and not interfere. Trying not
to feel like I'm waiting for him...

But I am.

DELETE

I knew what I had to do. I deleted you. I blocked you on every form of social media and contact platform. You'd been my ex for seven years and for some reason, even though you had broken my heart so many times, I couldn't let you go completely. This time I knew what I had to do. I couldn't face waiting to see if you would message me at 3 in the morning again. I ripped off the plaster of you for good. No contact. Once I did that, if I am being completely honest, you didn't even cross my mind. It was like you didn't exist anymore. The best thing I ever did was to say goodbye. Life is so much better with you completely gone.

UNSENT

Sometimes I enter your nickname in WhatsApp and type 'I miss you', just to get the words out of my head. I see the word 'online' appear, wishing for it to change to '... is typing'. As if you'll read my mind and say, 'I miss you too'. But just seeing you're online and OK has to be enough for now because you were right. We couldn't carry on.

IT HAD BEEN TEN YEARS SINCE I LAST SAW HER

We met in 2006, when we were naive to our feelings for each other. I fancied her, she fancied me, but we didn't act on it. We've talked about how the dates we had at the time were the best days of our lives, we just didn't know it then.

In the ten years since we last saw each other, we've been through it all. Every bad thing life can throw at you happened to us. Life was kicking us when we were down, but the things we've endured have made us strong individuals.

Last year, my ex broke off our engagement. It sent me spiralling into depression and anxiety because of her massive web of lies and deceit. I struggled to cope. The pressures of life overwhelmed me, and I withdrew for months. I got through Christmas and started to feel better about myself. I bought into the 'New Year, New Me' vibes. I started to enjoy life again.

After having had a break from social media, I reactivated my accounts and started adding people again. I thought to look her up and see how she had been all these years. I messaged her asking how she was. Before I knew it, we were talking all day, our messages getting longer and longer as we really opened up to each other about our lives.

Very quickly, the romance started to pour. We video called each other, and it was amazing to see her beautiful face again. We met up, walked her dog in the park, held hands and kissed. It all came flooding back from when we first met fourteen years ago, but this time we were open about our feelings. We loved each other from the start.

It happened on April 16th. Girlfriend. Boyfriend.

We would find any excuse to leave our respective houses just to have five minutes with each other. I dreamed of kissing her all day long. I never took a single second for granted. The feeling I had the first morning I woke up next to her was indescribable.

I could fill books about what she means to me, how gorgeous she is, all the things we've done, but in the shortest time (or longest time, if you go back to 2006) we've fallen madly in love with each other and know that this is it forever. We're moving in with each other next month and I can't wait, because the sun rises and sets with her.

MY ROCK

I feel you like a rock in my shoe. It hurts me like you've hurt me too.

EVERY CELL

You're still the most handsome man I've ever met.

Once upon a time, about ten years ago, you were mine and I was yours. I'd only just moved to London and every day with you was an adventure, every small thing full of life. But I wasn't from the same background as you. And I was a feminist. It broke us.

Were you, are you, my person? I'd convinced myself you're not, that it never would have worked. For a long time now, I've felt OK about it all. And then the weirdest thing happened.

I was out on a walk and I was daydreaming about you, about what it would be like to see you again, half wondering whether that spark would still be there. And then, out of nowhere, you said my name, and I turned around and you were there. We walked, we sat, we talked. We talked until it was dark.

At the end, you hugged me, and I felt like I was home. It had been over seven years since we hugged like that, and my body still knew. Do you know that every cell in the human body replaces itself every seven years? So there weren't any cells left in either of our bodies that should have known the other from before. But mine knew.

You said we'd hang out. You didn't contact me. I didn't make contact either.

Then it happened again (seriously, universe?!). I was walking, thinking about you, and you appeared on the street in front of me. It felt so surreal. This time, we arranged to go for coffee. It felt different to sitting in the park, more restricted. I wasn't sure. But when we said goodbye, we hugged, just for a second, and my whole body came alive. Not alive like I just want to have sex with you, but alive like every cell in my body was conscious, happy and ecstatic to be home. It's hard to explain.

Again, we said we'd hang out. Again, neither of us has since made that happen. I think I'm OK with it – I'm not sure we are right for each other after all – but what if my body is right? What if you *are* my person?

Do you feel it too? Does it even mean anything?

BIG FEELINGS
We broke up five years ago, after dating for three months. I still think about you every single day. I just found out

you're getting married. On my birthday. I don't know how or where to start moving on. The worst thing is: I ended it because I was scared about the big feelings I felt. I knew this would happen one day, and it hurts so much more than I ever expected it would.

IT HAD BEEN TEN YEARS SINCE I LAST SAW HIM

I met him in 2006 when I was eighteen. He was this great force that burst into my life. He had the most beautiful eyes I had ever seen. Every word he spoke I took as gospel. We connected instantly and I was smitten.

Unfortunately, we lost touch over the years. Life happened, ten years went by. I lost my parents and had two children, and got stuck in an abusive relationship. From time to time, I found myself thinking about him. I wanted to know how he was, I wanted to hear his voice again. Did he think of me? Was he happy?

When I got that message from him, my heart was pounding. I instantly knew in that moment that this was the right time; it was now or never. I breathed him in, took down my walls and we connected just as we did all those years ago. That great force of a man I once knew was back in my life and like fuck was I letting him go again! I had loved him all along.

Now he's here with me, and with my children and loving us all. This kind, selfless and passionate soul that brings energy and life into any room he walks in. He has brought me back to life in every way possible.

And I get to look into those beautiful eyes – every, single, day.

LETTING GO

I just don't know how to let you go.

NORMAL PEOPLE

I've been watching *Normal People* with my ex-boyfriend. We live in different countries now, so all the watching is separate, followed by emails that might arrive in the recipient's inbox at about 3 a.m. their time. It's the perfect show to watch alone together: the soundtrack would be ruined by anyone else's live commentary, and aspects of the plot mimic our on-off relationship before I moved away and met someone better. We don't have in-depth discussions; an email might be a single sentence. I realize in writing this that I'm just so bored and lonely that this passes as entertainment. I used to be an interesting person and now I'm not. I don't care about the ex, who treated me badly while we were together, and wouldn't mind if he never emailed me again, but for now, all I've got is *Normal People*.

EVERYTHING HAPPENS FOR A REASON

I was heartbroken when he texted me saying he needed a break and, just like that, I never heard from him again. Two years later, I get a phone call from him asking me how I am.

I'm fine thank you, it's a shame you weren't this concerned two years ago when you broke my heart. I asked him why he did what he did and what the real reason for the phone call was.

I asked him never to call me again. I just wouldn't be able to cope with the pain he caused me in the first place. He begged me to give him another chance.

Everything happens for a reason. I am moving on now with my closure.

URBAN LEGEND

Well, the story goes... she went on a dating app for the first time ever, matched with her high-school boyfriend (who was her first ever kiss), went on some dates, fell in love, and is now living happily ever after!

IT WAS ALWAYS MEANT TO BE YOU

We reconnected after years apart. We'd been best friends for five years. We always knew we loved each other, but stupidly we didn't let the other know and went our separate ways. After you reached out, I saw you for the first time in almost seven years. My heart skipped a beat and I've had butterflies ever since. It was always meant to be you.

'I DON'T WANT A GIRLFRIEND'

I'd never really stopped thinking about you since we dated. You slid into my DMs right at the point when

I'd gotten over the fact that we were never going to get in touch again. We met and instantly there was a comfortable familiarity. It was so nice to be spending time with you, older and – I thought – wiser.

'I don't want a girlfriend,' is what you said. I respected that.

You slept with your ex.

I couldn't say anything, could I? Because you 'didn't want a girlfriend'.

You reintroduced me to your friends, asked me to go on holiday with you. We spent countless nights staying up talking into the early hours. I asked you out for dinner and you said, 'I don't want a girlfriend'.

Your mixed messages drove me crazy. I snapped. You went silent. You unfollowed me from Instagram.

Older and wiser? You're still a child and I stupidly fell for you again. I feel like a fool, used by you. I should have known better. 'Leopards don't change their spots,' as you once said to me.

DARK PARADISE

I lie here every night and I listen to Lana Del Rey, and I drink whiskey and I do everything I fucking can not to text you. What is it about being at home and alone that makes me want to run directly back into your arms?

CHEATED

You cheated on me and now you're engaged to her. How did you treat me like shit and get the happy ending that I can't seem to find? I hate that I still miss you.

WALKING

Bumping into you after all these months just confirmed it... you mean nothing to me now. I carried on walking like you were just a stranger.

WHEN?

We had a fling. I was totally obsessed. You were a marine doing whatever (and whoever) you fancied. Work gave you the excuse to stop seeing me, but you kept in touch every now and again just to boost your ego. I know all this and yet I can't let you go.

I read back the messages that are entangled with lies. If only I could take my mind off you and finally remove the rose-tinted glasses. I wish that you could give me the chance to turn you down, let me be the one who is done with it all. But instead, I'm the one who's craving more, feeling lost, and wondering how many years this heartache will last.

When will I be able to see your face pop up and not feel the beats in my chest quicken? When will your double-tap no longer be the main driving force behind every post? When?

IT HAD BEEN TEN YEARS SINCE I LAST SAW HER: PART 2

Bags packed, I moved in with her. I feel complete. Mam cried, but she loves that I'm the happiest I've ever been.

Tonight we're going to our favourite restaurant in the world. We're going to drink, eat, laugh, have fun and it's going to be this way forever. The dream became our reality. I didn't think I'd enjoy anything again after last year, but the intimate nuances you create as lovers mean that every single second is beautiful.

Tell me life was this great a year ago and I would call you a liar.

SEE ME

After breaking up with me and breaking my heart, two months later I'm still nowhere near healing and think of him every hour of every day. I text him weekly, begging him to see me, trying to sound happy and light-hearted in the texts instead of angry and upset. I asked him if there is any chance for us, or whether I should go back to the dating apps. He said there could be a chance and agreed to meet me the following week to 'see how we feel.' I already know how I feel, I love him and miss him like crazy.

I was excited to see him, hopeful that I'd change his mind – imagining how I'd fall into his arms.

The week dragged by, and, on the day, I texted to ask where and when we'd meet. He replied saying he was busy, but we would meet soon.

I was devastated. Another week passed so I texted again, asking if we were still meeting up. I remained hopeful, but have received no response. Why does he mess with me like this? It's cruel and unfair.

I'm now going to therapy. I know I need to move on, but I'd do anything to have our relationship back to how it was when we were so in love.

CRASH

A few years ago, we were together but drifted apart because of work commitments, so we broke up. Then we crashed into each other on a bike ride. Literally. He says it was coincidence, but he hasn't lost his balance on the bike since then.

We ended up having a drink by the river, and with him now off work, it opened a whole new chapter for us. We've spent more time together in the past few months than we had in all those years before. We both re-evaluated our priorities and realized that the only thing we truly want is each other.

I have now forgiven him for my bruised kneecap that day, as he's promised that he'll make it up to me by one day getting down on his!

26 YEARS LATER

I reconnected with a guy that I loved when I was fifteen years old. I spent the summer of 1994 visiting the café where he worked. We went on one date, then I never heard from him again. The pain was unbearable.

He messaged me last week. Told me he was an idiot for not noticing me before. Said I was beautiful. 26 years later, he's broken my heart again. My life sucks right now.

WITHOUT THE EX

After a long and tumultuous relationship (and a very protracted break-up) we finally, after two years, stop talking. Completely.

It turns out that the experience was like throwing open the windows in springtime and shaking the cobwebs out. It leaves a lot more space for light. I'm seven dates in with a lovely man who, even if it doesn't work out with, I feel happy to have known at all.

The ex has met someone too. Who knew you should stop talking to them?

THESE STORIES

Reading all these stories; I always find myself wondering if one of them is about you.

Some very clearly aren't. Some could be.

I know none are about me.

IT WAS ALWAYS MEANT TO BE YOU: PART 2

It is our first anniversary in a week. It's not been an easy year, getting through the challenges life has thrown us, adjusting to each other's needs and wants, blending our chaotic lives together. But we still make time for us. To go on adventures and share our favourite places. You've returned after working a week away and I missed you like crazy. My heart still skips a beat every time you walk through the door. Forever will be you.

I WISH

I wish I didn't miss you.

A MOMENT IN TIME

We hooked up at university. We'd always stayed in touch from a distance, and I always wondered about what might have been. We had been back in touch for a few months when lockdown happened and I found myself stranded – not in the country or city I normally lived in, but the city where he lived. The odd text in the months leading up to the pandemic turned into late-night phone calls that lasted hours.

We both lived alone and had been following strict social-distancing rules. We decided to take a calculated risk and break them. I cycled for over an hour to get to his place and this became our weekend routine.

It goes without saying that a pandemic was a surreal and poignant time to be experiencing new – or in our case, renewed – intimacy with someone. In the early stages of a relationship, you are always so engrossed in each other, but the empty streets outside really did make it feel like we were the only two people in the world. Exploring our minds, exploring our bodies, coping together, listening to music, cooking, reading the news, chastising the government, hoping for a revolution, getting drunk. Our university years made it instantly so familiar, so warm, so comforting – when comfort was desperately needed.

We both knew there was an end point; our closeness was to be fleeting. I would return to my city, in a different country, when restrictions lifted. Without needing to speak about it in any depth, we both knew that we wanted it to be something that only existed in that moment. A little make-believe relationship that would be frozen in time.

The 'new normal' began and I went home. We spoke occasionally for a few weeks, and then stopped. It didn't carry through into the new world; we left it behind. The creation of our little corner of the Earth at a time when it was still. Lockdown lovers.

IT HAD BEEN TEN YEARS SINCE I LAST SAW HER: PART 3

For me personally, last year should have been the best year of my life, and it was until a week ago.

The positive pregnancy test she showed me last Tuesday means that this year is now already the best, no matter what happens.

I'm going to be a dad!

YOU REMINDED ME

Just a few days after I had a fleeting moment of missing him, of believing life would be better with him around me, he messaged. After twelve months of silence, it's like my thoughts called him out of the woodwork.

For a moment, I thought he was finally ready to talk, to listen and to heal. I quickly realized my optimism; the conversation was going to be no different to all the conversations of the past. His dialogue was filled with anger, resentment and blame. I felt mine was filled with honesty, compassion and integrity.

While the dialogue was predictably familiar, there was one pivotal difference. This time his words washed over me. My heart didn't become heavy to his hate. I no longer felt sad that he couldn't see me for who I am. Instead, my heart felt light and joyous in the confirmation that walking away sixteen months ago was the best decision I ever made. My sadness was only for him, and the pain disguised as anger that he can't move through and let go of.

Thank you for the reminder that being alone may get lonely at times, but solitude is better than being with someone who claims to love you but really has far too much unresolved pain to love themselves, let alone anyone else.

MOVIE STYLE

I dreamt about my love last night. It was one of those intense, movie-style dreams where everything is so real.

He died in 2015. I sit on the bench I had dedicated to him in the local park and remember not only the dream I had.

AT THE VERY START

I went on a night out and bumped into my childhood crush on the dance floor. We lived on the same street from birth until I was 13. I hadn't seen or heard from him for 8 years, yet I knew his face as soon as I saw him, and he knew mine.

We got inventive with dates... sitting in the car playing our favourite songs, park walks, driving to the hills to watch the sun set and talking about our childhood memories. I found out that he had the biggest crush on me during our years growing up together... which I never knew! We fell deeply in love. Now we are together, everything is perfect.

Sometimes the person meant for you was there at the very start.

IT HAD BEEN TEN YEARS SINCE I LAST SAW HER: PART 4

You're early. You weren't supposed to be here yet.

You broke your mam's waters just over four weeks ago and you drove us into panic! Now here you are.

I'm honoured by your presence, enamoured by your beauty and totalled by your love.

I want the world that David Rose envisioned for you. A world of inclusivity, full of passion and devoid of hate. A world exhaustive of love sempiternal. A world that amplifies peace, happiness, affords every and all opportunities, and rewards kindness – and I'm going to give that to you.

I looked at you and realized that all the possessions and materials I have are insignificant, as nothing I have or create will ever change how beautiful the moment was when I heard you cry for the first time. My world has changed forever.

Seven weeks, six days early, but as stubborn as me and your mam, healthy and happy.

I MISS HIM

I miss him and there's nothing I can do.

THE BOY FROM 1949

I'm in my eighties.

I knew him when he was a 14-year-old boy in 1949. We both got married to other people, raised separate families. The boy searched for 57 years to find out what happened to me, 'the girl who moved away and changed her name' (because she got married). There was only one of our classmates who knew where I was. They put us in touch – and we sent Christmas cards to each other for about ten years.

Then, for five years after my husband passed, there was no contact. Eventually, I called him to enquire about the missing Christmas cards – thinking he might be gone. He said he'd wanted to give me time to grieve.

After that phone call he has been calling me 3-4 times a day. My life has a new beginning.

IT WAS ALWAYS MEANT TO BE YOU: PART 3

Fast forward and it's been almost two years since we reunited; full of love, laughs and tough times. I always chose you, fought for you and defended you because I thought you were my forever.

You chose someone else and didn't even think about me at home waiting for you. Why was it always you when it was never me?

IT'S NOT YOU, IT'S ME

Every now and then I meet a guy who texts like you. Every now and then I realize that there's no one like you. That's when I find myself scrolling through our old messages; finding myself still laughing over them, still feeling the flow, still loving our connection. That's when I realize how much I loved who I was when I was texting with you.

CAN WE? (MY ONE LOVE: UPDATE)

After months and months, he broke up with his girlfriend about a week ago. We made plans for him to come stay at mine for the Bank Holiday. We agreed we would take the time together to work out if something was there.

He's due to arrive on the Friday. On Monday, he tells me that he's slept with someone new and wants to see if there's a relationship there, but he hopes we can still be friends.

Can we fuck.

SINGLE

Much like its opposite, being single can feel by turns like a blessing or a curse. It can be fun, and wild, and free, but it can be tough given that we live in a world that still holds up romantic love as the goal, the pinnacle, the happy ending in the story. And sometimes you just really want a hug... or a fuck. When you don't know when that will next happen, it can feel frustrating and preoccupying.

But being single allows a total commitment to the self. Without the need to factor in a romantic partner, there is less need to compromise. What *you* want can become the focus and driving force of your life. To be single by choice is incredibly empowering.

There is a kind of super-strength that comes from being on your own, and not just surviving, but thriving. Knowing that, at the end of the day, you are the only resource you need might just be the biggest resource you'll ever have. Being independent and enjoying your own company means you're less likely to settle for an unfulfilling partnership.

Of course, at times, it can feel profoundly lonely. While we still live in a society that marks the timeline of lives with relationship milestones – getting married, having children – remaining single can make you feel like you are missing out on life; that time is passing and you are not fulfilling supposed life goals. Self-doubt and comparisons to others can creep in.

There is a lot of toxic positivity, aimed especially at single women, around self-love. Though not the aim, it can make people feel shame for wanting to find a romantic partner; that you just don't love yourself enough and need to do more 'work'. The messaging is that having sufficient self-love means that to be single should not be experienced as failure, yet our society still holds coupled status as the norm. These conflicting messages make it almost impossible to navigate single life without feeling that you are in some way falling short – but also embarrassed to admit you feel that way. Added to this there is, for some, the time-sensitive reality of wanting children, which means being single comes with a whole other set of questions, pressures and decisions.

These stories explore this complex reality: from the freedom and pride of living life on your own terms, the joy of putting yourself centre-stage, to the ambivalence and longing of being single, the self-doubt, the comparisons, and the harder, darker moments of being alone.

STILL SINGLE

Single. Single. Single. Single. Single. Single. Single. Single. – Ooh? No. Single.

I HAVE NEVER

I'm twenty-seven; never been kissed or kissed someone. Never been touched. Never been the one someone has chosen to love. The thing is, I know I'm not repulsive. I have options, I have a great job, a good family, a good house, I work out. The problem is, I have an innate fear of intimacy. I lie to all my friends and tell them I've had one-night stands and all this experience when in fact my experience tank is empty. I have a fear of someone looking too closely, seeing all my imperfections: the brokenness. On the surface, everything is shiny and unbreakable, but on the inside I'm paranoid, anxious and frightened. I met someone online and I thought for the first time: maybe this is it, this is what I have been waiting for all my life. How sad things turned out to be when he transpired to be another fleeting ship, sailing into the arms of another. So here I am, I continue to wait... kiss-less, sex-less and love-less.

INSPO

Everyone tells me that I'm succeeding. That I'm inspiring them to pick themselves up off the floor, dust themselves off, and go and get what they want. Over the past eighteen months I've worked a brilliant job, been made redundant, had a crisis, picked up a dream job at one of my favourite places, and am now working towards doing what I have dreamed of for years. I'm surrounded by the most wonderful family and friends. They all tell me to never change. That I'm bossing it exactly as I am.

But the truth is, I feel the opposite. I keep comparing myself to my friends, because so many of them are in relationships, getting engaged, getting married. They're happy and contented with someone. And I know that this shouldn't be a comparison I'm making. But it is, and I am. I've spent the last year realising that I can't make impermanent connections, that any frisky fun I have has to be remotely, with a stranger... because I've ended up catching feelings for the people that I know. Yes, multiple people, multiple genders. That was a fun realisation, too. There have been too many conversations, names mentioned, then lost connections.

Is it so wrong to want to be loved?

YOLO

I am working on loving myself and enjoying every minute of it. So far, so good. I have made a bucket list of all the things I want to do before I die. I've realized you only live once and that I need to enjoy my life. I need to live for me, need to prioritise myself – stop worrying about making everyone else happy and what other people think. When it comes to loving me, it only matters what I think.

I am responsible for me. I have decided to face my fears. I have always loved to sing, so I have joined a band.

Go me! I have finally got my ears, nose and helix pierced (have always wanted to). What was stopping me? I've also started to slow down. I spent two hours sat still, relaxing and painting my nails. I didn't feel guilty. I have started spending money on myself. Treating myself to a new coat and some jewellery. New sexy underwear. Just for me. I enjoy my own company.

I have stopped over-analysing everything. I have stopped looking too far ahead and too far back. I am loving living in the present!

SEX DREAMING

I've had a huge increase in dreams, usually involving ex-lovers, but also colleagues and other random assorted cast members. The dreams have been, almost exclusively, overtly sexual. I wake up most mornings with a sense of longing – only *just* overtaken by the more pressing need to make myself come. I need to feel something inside me, and the dreams leave such lingering images and a sense of touch I am sorely missing. I just want to be touched. At this point, I don't even care who by. Who will be the next one to touch me? I may explode.

FULLY LOVE

I very recently fell out of love and broke up with my partner.

Being single has led to many thoughts and self-reflection. And I realized I need to fully love and support myself before I can be with anyone in a good way.

WHAT I WANT

After many an evening spent frantically rushing home from work to shower, then rushing back out to meet Jack from Hinge at Gordon's Wine Bar, I've been thinking. I've spent hours critiquing my thoughts, dreams and desires; combing over my sexual history with my therapist. I've asked myself what I actually want from life and discovered a lot.

I no longer want a conventional, monogamous relationship. I no longer want to have children. I want to explore my sexuality, date women and men, go to sex parties and have multiple lovers. I've been celibate for months, and it's freed me from the shackles of my 'biological clock' – of the incessant desire to find 'The One' and of the conventions of a 'normal relationship'. My eyes have been opened to a world that I never thought I'd have the strength to become part of. I'm excited. I feel more liberated and in control than I ever thought possible when it comes to my expectations and desires, and dreams for love.

MY BEST LIFE

Crushing break-up. Moving away to uni. Reality hitting. Sleeping around. Crying. Fear.

Excitement for a vibrant future. Falling in love with myself and a new city. But still under the unshakeable control of negative emotions months on.

Attempting to meet up with the ex in our hometown. Clawing at a friendship. Refusal on their part. Realising that their presence contributes only negative energy.

Finally beginning to genuinely move on. Happiness and stability come slowly crawling back. Being forced to move home. Scared to lose my progress. Worry.

Devastating return of the poor mental health I feared so much. Struggling to deal with the rawness of painful memories that never quite managed to fully heal.

Trying to reach out again. Knowing this only makes things worse. Finally ceasing contact.

Bad times. The incessant bad dreams won't stop, despite my forward steps. Attempting to explain my state of mind to worried family. The arguments.

What about therapy? I wouldn't know where to start.

Reclaiming my space. Disgusting Tinder matches. Tinder matches that go nowhere. Ten promising talking stages always ending with disappointment.

Trying to embrace my position. Wanting to romanticise my position. Losing motivation and any sense of direction.

Guilt. Never escaping the over-thinking of past decisions and events.

A promising and different feeling Tinder match followed by an accidental hook-up. The return of stability and an exciting and fulfilling connection? It didn't go anywhere, of course it didn't! It was only casual, silly! The kind of casual where mutual respect and communication are optional extras. The ever-present spiral of nit-picking at my own characteristics and searching for the reasons behind every single rejection. Not wanting to need another to feel validated ironically doubled alongside my inability to escape the clutches of the very human need for intimacy.

Manic phases and random blocking sprees. Once again linking all failed connections to the original lost lover. Why can't I stop talking about it? I want to but I just can't.

Anger and paralysing jealousy of happy couples, especially those of my dearest friends. Questioning the morality behind my own futile frustrations.

Feeling like a fucking child in my family home and I can't get away. How to get help? Scary.

Too many thoughts all the time. Confusion and frustration have outstayed their welcome. I don't think it's formative anymore. This wasn't the plan; I was supposed to be living my best life.

I move back to uni next week. Relying on a change of scene and not so long-off change of situation so I can finally thrive in the way my long-ago-self used to.

THE SAME

Haven't had sex for two years.

NO MORE COMPARISONS

I found myself feeling lost, not because he left (to be honest, it's probably the best thing he's ever done for me), but because I was desperate to fill the hole of being in a relationship.

I dated and it took me on an emotional rollercoaster: the highs when someone showed interest, the lows when it didn't go anywhere. I didn't know what I was looking for, just someone. I didn't embrace being single, I felt like it wasn't normal. I compared myself to people my age having children, getting engaged or getting married.

Then it hit me. It's OK to be single. I'm not ready to jump back into a relationship months after a break-up... even if he has. I'm now learning to be back in control of my happiness. I feel content and I'm bouncing back to feeling myself again.

Being in the wrong relationship is exhausting, that's what isn't normal. So thank you, but I'll wait.

SO-LO

It's been nearly five years since a man has touched me. I have been so lonely that there have been moments that I have wanted to curl up and die. But I've learnt how to truly love myself and make love to myself. Also, I've had someone to dream about; someone I fell for a long time ago who didn't feel the same. He contacts me occasionally (probably when he's desperate) and I am proud of myself for not falling for his charms again, but I really appreciate having my fantasies about him because it is too dark not to have anyone to think about.

Now when I go for walks, I smile more at everyone, not just men. I never expect a smile back, but when it happens it's wonderful and it's enough. Short conversations with strangers make me smile, I am blessed to have my health, and nature is beautiful. I love my family, my granddaughter is my world, and I still hope to share this love with someone who wants to receive it.

Also, I bought myself a bright pink rabbit vibrator. Happy fanny.

MY OWN

After more than thirty years of living with family, friends and housemates, for the first time ever I've found myself living alone. And I am in love! I'm in love with dancing around the place in my underwear, with singing aloud and not caring how awful I sound, with being able to make a space fully my own, with all the possibilities it brings. I guess, ultimately, I'm in love with being able to live a lifestyle that's fully my own, where I can put my needs and wants centre-stage for once – it's been a long time coming!

A YEAR OF ME

We were together for three years. I was always in love with the man he could be, not the man who was in front of me. He was a violent binge drinker, but I excused it all. He moved in and, eleven months later, my neighbour called the police as his drinking and violence had steadily increased until he tried to strangle me. The police intervened and took him away, and I have never seen him since. Enough was enough.

Now for the love story: I rebuilt my relationship with myself. I spent a year reading and learning about my cyclical behaviour with fucked-up men. I exercised, ate better, threw myself into work, got a puppy (almost as stressful as a violent drunk man, but not quite), worked some more, spent time alone – properly. I went to therapy, got a personal trainer, and fell back in love with myself. I've never been more content with my life, never been more connected to my friends and family, and most importantly have never been more confident that I won't walk that path again.

You can get out of terrifying situations; you can break the cycle and you can be free. Feeling like a queen and celebrating with champagne – it's been a year of falling in love with me.

JUST FINE

Single and living alone. Honestly, I can't think of anyone else I'd rather spend this much time with. We're told to judge ourselves harshly, to hold ourselves to account, to compare ourselves to what's expected. This time alone has taught me that I'm doing just fine, and there's no shame in taking pride in who I am.

AS RU PAUL SAID

I made the decision to fully delete all my dating app profiles. This was a difficult decision as I'd been single for four years.

I decided that the energy I was spending on dating apps, having average conversations with average men, was valuable energy that I could be investing in myself.

I've tried to put that energy into new hobbies, existing friendships and future plans.

There is so much pressure on relationships and finding 'The One', but as Ru Paul said, 'if you can't love yourself how in the hell you gonna love somebody else?'.

I guess my love story hasn't been as simple as girl meets boy; my story has been falling back in love with me, myself and I.

ANYONE

Is anyone else just reading these stories single AF? Fully accepting it may never happen.

MY LIFE

I miss her so much. The happy, friendly, loveable girly girl. Where did she go? She left her dream job, started a business and put self-centred men on a pedestal. She listened to words rather than actions and over-explained herself over every small matter.

I'm reflecting as a shell of my former self.

Next month I've booked a one-way ticket to Europe, to find the glitter, the sunshine and the zest to my life again. I am taking control for my twenty-nine-year-old self to live a life of confidence and joy; to say goodbye to depression, to living in four walls, and narcissistic men. I'm choosing me this time. I'm scared, anxious, and my feelings are raw – but if I can do this, then you can too.

One life and there's no return and no deposit.

GIFTED

I am a single mum. Last Christmas was my first Christmas alone and I had no presents to open. So, this year I have bought and wrapped my own presents. Don't feel sorry for me. I've given myself some really nice gifts! Much better than any of the presents my ex would have bought me. This year it's all about self-love.

FAKE IT TIL YOU MAKE IT

My relationship ended. We were never right for each other, but I've never loved anyone so much.

After eight or nine years of truly hating myself and never feeling like I was good enough, pretty enough, smart enough, too sensitive and too intense, I decided I didn't want to be like that anymore. I thought I'd never find love again. I couldn't imagine another person even wanting to kiss me. But I built myself up and just pretended I thought I was fine. And as it turns out, if you pretend enough it starts to become real anyway and other people believe it.

I also realized that there's a lot to be said for the space in between. Love isn't a relationship, or waiting for a proposal, or moving in together. There's significant love and life that exist completely independently of all that and just because it's not 'official' doesn't mean that it isn't significant.

After feeling like I was never going to be in love again or be loved again, I started to see a change and realized I could see love all around me in completely different forms to how I'd ever thought about it before. Because I saw this in other people, I started to see it in myself too. I realized how important those connections are, even if they are tenuous, and that I wanted to live my life fully loving other people in any form they came in. And loving myself too.

TIME

Time to breathe
    Time to think
    Time to organise
    Time to reflect
    Time to look at my photos
    Time to phone my aunt and listen to her long stories
    Time to get to know my neighbours
    Time to see the sun move across the sky
    Time to read
    Time to cycle
    Time to walk the dog – the long way round
    Time to cook a healthy dinner
    Time to plan what's next!

DANCING ON MY OWN

Alone and sad, in spite of my traditional profession, I decided to have dance classes. Now I am a doctor and a pole dancer. I am proud of both. My videos dancing and my pics at work are on Instagram. This year was a time for self-love and courage.

SELF-LOVE

I watch more porn than I would ever care to admit.
Along with taking endless pictures of my tits.

FIERCE

After a year of dating aggressively, of trying desperately
to fill my own emptiness with the company of another,
I took time to realize that I'm okay on my own. After
dating a guy who brought another girl from a dating app
to a party I was at with him, I decided enough is enough,
and stopped.

I learnt to fill my time with things other than
swiping for hours on the apps. My head wasn't filled
with obsessed thoughts about the lives of men who
couldn't care less about mine, and I finally had a sense
of freedom. Fast forward four months and I have new-
found fierce independence. It makes up for the year of
ghosting, mindless sex and rejection. I learnt how to love
myself.

NICE

I think I'm finally understanding that being alone is
better than being with the wrong one. I used to have
to dim my light for someone who had a fragile ego. Be
funny enough to entertain friends, but not funnier than
him. Be pretty, but not attract other guys' attention.
Be clever to charm a family dinner party, but not more
intelligent than him.

I hope he finds a nice girl who is nice enough to enchant, but not steal his limelight. Good luck to them. That'll be... nice. I want more than 'nice'!

SOUND OF SILENCE

I've always loved music; I would listen to it all day if I could. But I'd never noticed the 'in between' time – getting my phone out, searching for my favourite artist (JP Cooper), putting my headphones in. Anything up to the point before I press play. But now it's very apparent – unbearable, in fact. Silence. What did I do before, what went through my head? Time with myself, just me. No thank you. I did anything I could to avoid silence. It was deafening. When my alarm would go off I'd leave it on until I'd found my next podcast episode or music playlist. Pathetic really, not to mention annoying for my housemate. This lasted a while and everything I used to love listening to became stale, tarnished.

One day in the months following this, I went out on one of my favourite walks. The sun was out and everything looked brighter. But suddenly, my headphones died and it was silent. I felt it coming and couldn't stop it – there I was crying, in broad daylight. I thought to myself 'I'm fine. I'm always fine... aren't I?'. But, this wasn't the first time the crying had crept in. I wasn't fine, that was more than apparent now. I sat down on a bench on a beautiful day, with tears rolling down my cheeks and I knew something had to change. Reaching for my phone, I looked up an email a friend had politely given me a few weeks earlier of someone to speak to. (I'm not sure why I didn't take this as a hint earlier on, but all in good time.) And in that moment, in silence, I wrote an email reaching out for help that would change my whole world.

I now have love for myself, for music once again. And I tell you what – the occasional silence is bloody lovely.

I THINK I MIGHT BE LIVING MY BEST LIFE (MY BEST LIFE: UPDATE)

I was right and I couldn't be happier about it. Moving back to uni brought me everything I could have hoped for. A year of instability finally reached its end in ways I once never thought possible. I didn't expect anything to happen with anyone, and just by chance it did. These things always do when you're not looking for them, it seems.

I am truly happy, in part due to unexpectedly falling for someone who's been in my life for a year now. A hook-up-turned-casual-friends-with-benefits-turned-exclusive and now turned-blossoming-relationship. It's warm and healthy and I'm more than grateful. I don't feel dependent and am open and accepting of the complexities that the future brings our young selves.

I don't write this to boast – I don't feel smug at all. In fact, it pains me since I know the crushing feeling of reading of others' luck and happiness when it feels like your own world is falling to pieces. I've watched others, who seemed so content, while I was struggling. It's devastating. I write this from the other side, almost to tell my past self (and anyone else who needs it) that the most important thing to do is cherish and prioritise your sense of self. I'm not perfect, I still struggle. But if last year has taught me anything, it really is that you need to be the centre of your own narrative. Because when you are, things really slot into place.

SAME STORY

I have lost count of 'the almost relationships' I have had. I didn't sleep with any of them, but that's all they wanted in the end. Exhausted. Take a break and start again? I have done that each time.

How do you explain to family, friends, doctors who keep reminding me to 'get on with kids'? Why do they think I am not trying hard enough to find 'The One'? Why more pressure, as if I don't put that already on myself?

This year I thought maybe I'd met 'The One', but I'm slowly realising that he might be wedded to his work. It's been another year of getting to know someone, and another year of disappointment.

Thank you for hearing me out on this page, when my own friends are probably tired of lending me their ear on the 'same story again'. I feel too ashamed to pick up the phone to talk. It's as if something is wrong with me because they are all married with their 2.5 kids.

BADASS FEMINIST LOVE

Can I tell you about how I've finally fallen in love with myself? About how I've faced my insecurities and imperfections and now see them as a tangle of beautiful qualities in a beautiful person? How I threw myself into therapy and how I've buried myself in books on co-dependency, and attachment theory, and badass feminist texts on learning to love yourself in a capitalistic world that feeds off your perceived unworthiness?

Winding up single and alone used to seem like a failure. But being alone is a choice, and being alone doesn't mean you are without love. Being alone means rediscovering old friendships, strengthening platonic love, embracing new connections, and it especially means learning to love your own company. I wish I'd known that a long time ago.

I used to be full of heartbreak and anxiety, and now I am bursting with love and strength.

FALL

This autumn, she thought to herself with a smile, I'll let the leaves do the falling.

NOT FAKING

I've been single for eleven years. There has been the odd fling, the odd false start, plus more first dates than I can count – and then there was one who broke my heart. I'm comfortable with my own company now that I've lost the self-consciousness of my twenties. I'm always happy for others when I hear of their lucky love stories – I'm not bitter or scorned. But I'd be lying if I said I was one of those people who declares 'I love myself so that means I'm content on my own'. I do love myself, but I'm ready to let someone else in.

I'm a happy person, as a rule, am financially independent, and have great friends. I'm trying to focus on my passion project and write a book. I don't believe a woman needs romance to be happy – but I do believe that happiness is only real when it's shared.

I am a hopeless romantic. I crave it. I crave burying my face in the neck of that one person whose scent I'll never tire of, tasting their skin salt. I crave us laughing at things that aren't funny to anyone else. And so, resolving to remain optimistic, I've ventured into the dating world once again. But I just can't fake it, and hardly anyone makes me *feel*. I fear that lightning won't strike for another decade, but can't let myself linger on this thought because I have too much love to give.

I'm not always so melancholy. But for now, I'm exhausted.

OH HONEY

I'm going to need some more batteries. It's just me and my unhealthy commitment to Lovehoney from now on.

HOOKING UP

While casual sex would appear to be more readily available than ever – with apps facilitating hooking up with a right swipe – Gen Z are famously having less sex than any previous generation. We are technologically entwined – but physically, it seems, we may be less connected than ever.

The days of having to meet someone in person or wait for posted letters are long gone. Personal technologies can be used to (very) personal effect to aid our sexual encounters. We can instantly direct message, sext, send and receive images, video call, watch pornography, and use apps to connect us to strangers all over the world. But attraction is a multi-sensory process, and whilst our sex lives have changed greatly with the advent of personal technology, there is still no substitute for the physical. Sexting may heighten desire, but it can also increase frustrations when our encounters don't materialise beyond the screen.

While, undoubtedly, attitudes towards sex have become more liberal throughout the years, we still hold a lot of shame around sex: how much we want it, do it, how soon, with how many partners. We are sexual beings and sometimes what we want is purely physical, with no romantic connection. There should be no shame in that, nor in the expression and exploration of our desires. Our sexuality is a fundamental part of who we are and discovering what we like, or don't like, our kinks and fantasies are a way to connect to ourselves and better understand what gives us pleasure – something we are all entitled to.

At times, however, for some, sex and hooking up can become a way of trying to distract the self from feelings you wish to avoid: boredom, loneliness, disconnection. Hooking up can be an attempt to feel connection, an attempt to feel *anything*. The pursuit of pleasure becomes a short-term fix for a deeper, unresolved pain. These hook-ups usually emphasise what they're not, leaving us feeling even lonelier in their aftermath. In time, however, there is hope that they'll direct us towards what we truly want or need.

These are stories about casual sex and desire. They are stories of adaption and experimentation, of daring to move beyond comfort zones and of discovering new aspects of the self. They are stories of freedom, frustration and longing – of desires fulfilled and unfulfilled.

PLAYTIME

Thirty-eight and newly single. I wanted a relationship, but no one was quite tickling my fancy. Quite frankly I was bored of dates in the pub, ending with a kiss on the cheek or a disappointing shag.

I met one guy who suggested we try a sex club. I'd been to Killing Kittens and Torture Garden before, but I'd found them performative and posey – not quite me. I'd never partaken, but then again, I'd never been tempted. He was into the kink scene and wanted me to dress in latex to get publicly played with, spanked and fucked. Who was I to argue?

The first date was a small afternoon affair on a Sunday afternoon. While my parents were in church, I was covering myself in enough talcum powder to enable squeezing into my new latex body suit. I'd never worn rubber before, but it was surprisingly sexy. I teamed it with thigh-high boots and long latex gloves, then I was ready to go.

Walking through Soho, no one looked twice – God, I love London. My playmate showed me around. It was a nightclub essentially, with a dungeon out the back full of spanking tables, ropes, harnesses and swings. It was 1 p.m. and I could see a man being pegged by his girlfriend, a girl being tied up and teased and couples of all genders and cultures playing with each other. And you know what, it was funny. It wasn't serious, it was funny. I met (and shagged) some great people that night who I'm still pals with today.

The next time I went I was with two men. Both gorgeous and fun. This was a big event, so we had to

queue to get in before our outfits ͺ
and leather essential, no 'usual' clothͺ

NINE

It was huge. Thousands of people. Gerͺ
playing. Strippers, naked aerialists, men in rͺ
on stage doing various performances. There weͺ
'playrooms' with ropes and wooden crosses and haͺ ͺs
and whips around. There were people in gimp suits being
pulled on leads, bodies piled on top of each other exploring
new crevices, and women being spanked on stage. A man
in a wheelchair was being orally pleasured by two girls.
Another guy stood in a box with just his penis sticking
out of a hole – a sign pointing to it saying 'use me'. There
were women on women and men on men and all genders
on all genders. It was weird and magical and sexy and
disgusting and exciting... and it stank. Really stank. I could
get over the smell though because I wanted to get involved.

I got fucked by both of my playmates. Separately
and then at the same time. I got spanked by a German
dominatrix who made me scream with pleasure and pain
at the same time. I went into a dark room and let anyone
touch me. I met someone who called himself 'the human
toilet' – and that's exactly what he was that night. Not for
me. I just... no.

At 4 a.m. the lights came on as we queued for our
coats. I saw a man who I'd sucked off puking in the
corner, and a girl who I'd kissed screaming at the cloak
room attendant. I saw condoms on the floor and patches
of sticky liquid on every surface. I saw couples arguing
amongst bemused security guards. I thought, next time
I'll leave before the lights come on.

...in the past eighteen months I have dated nine different men. Each gained a nickname: PE Teacher, The Knob, Irish, Fireman, Hatfish, Danny Boy, The Plumber, Traveller and Scottish. Each one of them wanted a second date – but I didn't.

Two turned into flings and then into a 'friends-with-benefits' arrangement. One I spoke to every single day for six weeks, but when I finally met him, I spent the entire date thinking of everyone else I would rather have sex with. I am not even sure *why* I was dating now, maybe I just wanted to have sex.

I've deleted the apps and think I am going to decorate my house and buy a new vibrator as distractions. But I know when I get a quiet moment on my own, I will end up swiping to fill the void. There is still a part of me that craves connection.

WHAT I NEED

I've come to enjoy something that I never thought I'd have the guts to try: meeting with random strangers in parks and woodland. I'd enjoyed hook-ups in the past, but this way I'm able to cut out the bullshit and just get what I need. It's been an incredible experience and I've never felt more comfortable sexually than when experiencing those brief but intense moments.

However, I don't know how much longer I can continue engaging in such practices. The beautiful weather helped but now it's cooler I feel less inclined to bare all. I feel like I need to cut down but I know it's going to be difficult. I've found a new outlet. I will always want more.

UNICORN FEELDS

I decided to join Feeld; an 'alternative' dating app for the 'open-minded'. I wasn't exactly vanilla, I'd dabbled in light BDSM and had a couple of flings with the same sex, but this app introduced me to a whole new world of sexual experiences. Who knew a tickle fetish was a thing? Or foot jobs were so lucrative? Or being shagged while your hands are on the hobs of your stove? (Yup, really.) I've had my fair share of one-night stands, but I wanted something more adventurous, more exciting. I also didn't want the hassle of a relationship. I'd never heard the term 'unicorn', but it was an incredibly popular search on Feeld. It referred to couples looking for a female playmate to join them for some no-strings fun. I decided to go for it.

The first interaction was on a barge. As I was walking down the canal path and getting closer and closer to my destination, with trepidation in every step, I was wondering what this evening would bring. Awkwardness? Sex? Just chatting and a cuppa? I had no idea. We sat on top of the barge with wine and a spliff and talked a lot about Feeld and what they were expecting from this. It was their first time with a unicorn. They were excited. They wanted to mix things up a bit. I kissed her, he kissed me, we went inside. It was all fun and games until we were naked in bed and I'm suddenly taken out of the moment by the sounds of whimpering coming from the corner of the room. There ends this first adventure and the start of a common pattern – the boy wants a threesome and the girl *thinks* she wants a threesome until it actually happens. Leaving a weepy girl, a horny guy and me paying for an Uber home. Once home, my phone pinged; 'Sorry about that, she gets a bit jealous. Fancy meeting up just the two of us?' If he hadn't used the winky-face emoji, I might've been tempted.

The second interaction was in a pub. It was a hot summer's day. I skipped through the park to meet a gorgeous, local French couple. We had drinks and food and a very open conversation about how this was going to work. We went back to their place. God, they were sexy as hell. Clothes off, kissing, licking, biting – lots of delicious things until he starts fucking me from behind and I hear her say, 'I bet she doesn't feel as good as me.' I chose to ignore it but scarpered once the condom was off. He later texted me to ask if we could meet separately, saying he 'could come over to mine and his partner never needed to know about it'. Sigh.

My third experience was with a Spanish couple. That was fun. They wined and dined me and took me to extravagant hotels. They were older and wiser and interesting and intelligent. I fell for them a little bit. I think they fell for me. We went to Venice for a sexy weekend away and stayed in the hotel room ordering champagne and cheeseburgers. They then invited me to their family villa in Seville – yes please to a lovely week away. I imagined sunbathing and sex and swimming and sex and fine-dining and sex. What I hadn't imagined was that I'd be picked up from the airport by his aged parents and end up babysitting their niece. Yes, it turned out it was an extended family holiday and I'd somehow unknowingly become part of a thruple.

So that was it. My three threesome unicorn adventures. I didn't think I'd be doing that in my late thirties. Unicorns are a rare magical creature, but once the magic has gone, you're just an animal with a redundant horn.

PHONE SEX

4 girls on the go. 1 ex still lingering. 4 fake orgasms per night over the blower at staggered times. I'm the empty vessel. I make the most noise.

THE ITALIAN JOB

At the end of February, I matched with a gorgeous, much younger, Italian guy on a dating app. We met for a drink and instantly hit it off. He was charming, chatty and very intelligent. One drink turned into several over the course of five hours. The conversation never faltered, but I really didn't think he was attracted to me. There had been no playful arm touches or sneaky knee grabs.

When last orders were called, he asked if I was going to come home with him. I said I was at a 5/10 and, for me to come with him, he'd need to get me to 10/10. He made some remarks about me not regretting going with him. I teased that we hadn't even kissed, how could I possibly know if I wanted to have sex with him? He told me to put on my coat and that we were leaving. He grabbed my hand and started walking in the direction back to where he lived. I willingly followed.

Before we got too far, I reminded him that we still hadn't kissed, and I still wasn't at 10. He kissed me with such a force that my head started spinning (the rose wine had nothing to do with it). He asked, 'Was that good enough to get you to a 10?'. It most certainly was.

We got back to the shared house he was living in and entered a tiny bedroom. I saw the smallest single bed and thought to myself, 'WTF, he really thinks I'm going to shag him in that kid-size bed?'. He was 6ft 2in!

Turned out he had the largest penis I've ever seen and, 90 minutes later, the best sex of my life was over. We had sex one more time before he decided to return to Italy to be with his family. I was gutted that he left. But if he'd stayed in London, I know I would have fallen hard for him, and that was never an option. We still speak every few days and we're great friends. He will always be the best I've ever had.

AL FRESCO AFFAIR

Met a married man last month and have begun a very hot and steamy affair. We're exclusively having sex outside.

THE HOT GUY

I met a hot guy on the dating apps in February. We went on a few whirlwind dates and kissed in the front of his work van during a hail storm. It was a lot of fun before it tapered out.

I needed a new boiler and I put a shout-out on Facebook asking for advice. He was my friend on Facebook and happened to be a plumber, so contacted me suggesting that he could do it. He arrived at my house on a weeknight, chewing some gum, still in his work gear. We flirted, he gave me a great quote and we ended up kissing.

He returned a week later, we shared some chilli and nachos and he stayed the night. In the weeks afterwards, we would message occasionally but it fizzled out again. Then, after about three months, he returned to fit my boiler. We flirted a lot but kept a distance from each other. He promised to return to fit some radiators.

Three months later, he returned to fit the radiators. There was a lot of sexual tension and we ended up kissing on the sofa before going upstairs to rip each other's clothes off.

He forgot a part for the radiator and had to return on Friday to complete the job. He devoured me on the Chesterfield armchair in my front room.

This is the end of my love story.

SEX BUCKET LIST

At the beginning of March, my boyfriend of three years broke up with me out of the blue. We had been looking at houses to buy two weeks before, and I felt blindsided. After having to move in with my parents, it's safe to say I was forced to confront a lot of demons. Fast forward four months, having drinks with some girlfriends, they decided it was time for me to get back on the horse and created a Hinge profile for me. That's when I saw him. He was edgy and had this mysterious look about him; I wanted to know more. We matched but very quickly the next day, the influx of messages on the app sent me into a panic and I realized I wasn't ready for the dating scene. We'd already followed each other on Instagram and the conversation kept flowing. I felt more at ease knowing I had deleted Hinge and only had one person to reply to. He asked about my situation and understood I wasn't ready, so we carried on messaging just as friends.

Over the course of a month the chats got flirtier and flirtier, and the chemistry between us was undeniable. We agreed to go on a date, and being the first date I'd had in over three years, I'd say it went pretty well. We laughed, drank, spoke about our passions for travelling. We went back to his and I couldn't help myself, we slept together. It was the best first date I'd had in so long. After a week of messaging and failed attempts at planning a second date, he said he couldn't carry on, that he had lots of things on his mind and wanted us to stop before it got even more intense. I was confused, disappointed and hurt that the first person I'd really opened up to since the break-up had rejected me. I respected him for not completely ghosting me, which is usual in this day and age, but I left it. He then deleted his Instagram for me never to hear from him again.

Three months later he popped up, liking my posts on Instagram and replying to stories. He was back and the flirty messages continued. I decided I would use my new-found confidence and ask for what I wanted. The sex was great, he was comfortable – why couldn't we do fun and no strings? I definitely wasn't ready for a relationship, and the idea of a casual fling with him was a perfect scenario. A few weeks and naughty pictures later and we'd set a date – I'd come round to his and we'd start ticking things off our 'sex bucket list'. It was like a movie – I'm talking sex on the couch, carry-me-to-the-bedroom-type stuff. It was fun, surprising, exciting but comfortable at the same time. Afterwards we talked like old friends and watched a movie, then I left, not breaking my 'no-sleepover rule'. Like déjà vu, not even a week later, the dreaded paragraph landed in my DMs. 'I thought I could do no strings and just fun, but I can't. The sex is amazing but it isn't sitting well with me and I have a lot on my mind.' Like before, he wasn't giving anything away, no real reasons. Refusing to let me into his head. I still don't know what happened and I doubt I ever will. It could have been so much, but was never given the chance. It will always be the fling that never was. Did he catch feelings? Did I?

VAGINA DIALOGUES

We connected over a recipe exchange that his sister sent us. We emailed twice and then – nothing. His sister (my best friend) hinted that he might be into me (showed me messages where he said he found me attractive). I can't deny that inflated my ego. So, I sent him a limerick about my vagina and we went from there.

We met in a park the other day. I had been up all night and was exhausted. Luckily, he talks a lot so I could relax. And I did relax. He is easy to listen to. I can be quite an intense person – I give my all to everyone. I am worried that he thinks I want more from the situation than I do. We both said we don't want to be exclusive, but I don't know whether he is seeing other people. I am.

I hope it continues, but these types of situation always have an end point. It can't end badly for my friend/his sister's sake. I don't even know why I am thinking about it ending when it hasn't even begun! Chronic over-thinker.

Anyway, I keep dreaming about having sex. I actually masturbated thinking about him, which I never do (I always use porn). And now I can't stop thinking about his body. I am obsessed. I hope he has a good dick. If he doesn't, that would be a real shame.

THE HOT CHEF

For my friend's birthday in the summer, we celebrated by going for a meal at a bougie restaurant. Unusually for me, I was early and the first to arrive. While waiting for my friend, I noticed the hot chef working there. I stared at him all evening, but he was either completely oblivious or uninterested in my gazes.

At the end of the meal, our waiter came over and handed us two bills, one of which (mine) had a number and a kiss scribbled on it. I asked the waiter who it was from and was astonished when he replied, 'the ridiculously good-looking chef'.

I played it cool and didn't text him until the next day. It was clear from the start that he was interested in one thing only. I left it for a couple of weeks. I wasn't about that life. Then one idle Tuesday, feeling confident in my endeavours, I shaved, fake tanned, put on matching underwear and messaged him. 'I'm having dinner in East London tonight. Will you be about later?'. He replied within 20 minutes. 'Hey, yeah. That sounds perfect.' I was unsurprised that he had agreed. My gut told me he would.

I agreed to meet him at 10 p.m.. 10 p.m. came and I called him. It went straight to voicemail. My friend ordered the strongest cocktails the bar could provide, and we began to go into detail about how much of an arsehole he was. Five minutes later my phone lit up. 'I'll be there in 15 minutes' it read.

He came to meet me at the restaurant. When he arrived, he looked even more handsome than the first time I had seen him. I could barely look him in the eye. How was it possible that he found me attractive?

The drinks and conversation flowed, and I was surprised by how funny he was and how well we got on. What are the chances of someone you find attractive finding you attractive back and getting along? After our second drink he leaned in for a kiss. It was magical – our mouths and movements synched perfectly. At midnight, last orders were called. 'Would you like to see me again?' I asked tentatively. 'Yes,' he smiled back.

We left the bar. 'What would you like to do now?' he asked. 'We could go back to mine? Or to yours?' I debated – yes, and I might not see him again or he might not take me seriously; no, and I might not see him again and waste my shaved genitals and the chance of sleeping with a beautiful man. 'Let's go back to yours,' I decided.

We got an Uber back to his. I drank whiskey and listened to music half naked on top of him until 4 a.m.. Eventually we had sex. I was surprised how good it was. It felt so good and so natural – it was like he knew my body and vice versa.

In the morning, I woke up before him. I secretly reapplied my makeup in the bathroom and washed my mouth out with toothpaste, wondering whether we would have sex again – hoping we would. He made me a cup of tea in bed. He then kissed me on the lips, and then in between my legs until I came. 'Fuck,' he said, looking at the time, 'I'm going to be late for work.' He jumped in the shower and got dressed. He kissed me goodbye on the lips, 'See you later'. I showered, made the bed and cycled home, wondering whether I would see or hear from him again.

The next day came and went. Nothing. On Thursday my phone lit up. 'Hey, thanks for making my bed. It was really sweet of you.' My heart filled with warmth and joy. We texted back and forth for a bit. Then he left me on unread. I asked him out again three weeks later. He agreed straightaway but cancelled last minute – he had forgotten it was his grandma's birthday.

Three months later and one very drunken text exchange later cemented where I stood with him. He is seeing someone exclusively now. He revealed that 'that night was lit' and that he would like to see me again if he was single. I can't help but feel sad and wonder why it never worked out. I hope I'll see him again one day – or that the universe has other plans in store for me.

COOL

I want you to push me up against the fridge again.

THE AWAKENING

I was on a fourth (and final) date with a Hinge match when I woke up in his bed in a hot sweat after a dirty dream about someone else. It had been nine years since we'd seen each other, but I knew I had to tell him about it. One DM-slide later, and we're having regular phone sex and sending the kinkiest nudes ever. It's a sexual liberation.

DIRTY

Summer brought me a sexy Irish Bumble match. We have phone sex every night and he tells me I'm his 'wee dirty English slut', and honestly it makes me weak.

FUCK BOYS

I met someone on Hinge. We met up and got on really well. I ended up going back to their flat but hit it off harder with their housemate/best friend. I ended up staying the night and woke up with the horrific feeling that I'd just slept with a fuck boy. Some time later, the best friend confirmed my feeling and took the opportunity to tell me that *they* were actually into me. We had video sex and it was great. So fuck you, fuck boy. I've not seen or spoken to either since.

PLAY THING

I've been seeing this guy for about a month now. He's incredibly sexy, very manly and we have crazy sex. His main objective is to make me orgasm. He says he wants me to use him like a 'play thing'. After just coming out of a serious relationship, I didn't really know what to expect, nor did I know what I wanted. But I'm loving this single life – it's been great.

However, we were chatting today, and he said I was very 'Girl Next Door'. Instantly alarm bells started ringing – not only because he compared me to that awful archetype, but the fact that I'm solely using him for his cock and he hasn't noticed it.

LOVE HIGH

We shared a line of gear in the park on a bench at midnight, then we fucked all night long in the bushes.

ONE-NIGHT THING

End of February, and after talking to a guy online for a few weeks I had a 'why not' attitude and agreed to meet him one night. I hadn't been with anyone since my ex of ten years cheated on me a few months before. The sex was out of this world but I wasn't looking for anything serious, I just wanted to live a little. Not long after, he invited me over again, and so I regularly drove over late at night to spend time with him. Then we began to go on dates... and spend all our time together. Now I appear to have moved in. I never imagined that this would happen after that first night in February, but I really believe he is The One.

THREE WEEKS, 15 DICKS

In the space of three weeks, I amassed a total of 15 dick pics from various horny singletons around the capital. This provides a hilarious topic for my weekly catch-up with my friends, where they attempt to guess this week's number, which is quickly followed by an explosion of laughter when they realize how far off they all are.

The naughtiness continues through the apps, everyone desperately trying to subdue their raging sex drives with a little digital fun. I've considered a FaceTime session with a couple of men who were incredibly persuasive (and equally horny) but I chickened out last minute. How can I actually have sex with myself live on camera with someone I've never met? How do you start? Nice to meet you, here's my vagina?

BUILDING WITH BENEFITS

Early one Saturday morning, I was woken up by crows screeching outside my bedroom window. As I was lying there, willing them to fly away, I heard my upstairs neighbour's window open and a guy yell 'FUCK OFF!' to scare the birds away. The window was then slammed closed again.

A couple of hours later, I took his number from our building WhatsApp group and sent him a jokey, banter-y message thanking him for scaring off the crows. We had a laugh, which sparked a nearly constant stream of back-and-forth messages that lasted for days.

After a week, the tone in our messages turned cheeky and suggestive. We had basically both decided that we wanted to sleep with each other. We also only knew what the other looked like from our WhatsApp profile pics, so we shared a couple more photos each, and agreed to have a drink together on the Friday night, filling that wait with more chat and flirty texts. Friday, 7 p.m. – he came downstairs to my flat and within 5 minutes we were having sex. We quickly struck up a very convenient arrangement where a few nights a week we'd hang out and have sex.

We are both very clear we don't want a relationship with the other, having been far too honest in a lot of early conversations. We are the epitome of 'friends with benefits'.

BEAUTIFUL CREATURES

After ending a miserable and brief relationship in March, when my partner demonstrated zero ability to support me in my stress as a healthcare worker, I downloaded the dreaded apps again.

However, six months or so later, I now have a hareem of beautiful men to call on at a moment's notice. There's the stunning elf-like model, the talented and edgy music producer, the lovely but lost young Leo lookalike, a gorgeous and decadent classical pianist, plus various other lovely femme boys who come and go. Thank you to the dating app Gods for releasing these creatures to me!

Amongst the stress of work, I now have many delights to choose from.

TOO MUCH

We'd both had enough of trying to find love in this crazy world. I was getting over a bad break-up and you wanted sex. You were hot and cold. Making me feel like a million dollars when you had time, then leaving me on read in the next breath. I welcomed this distraction though, from the heartbreak I was struggling to get over, and would happily obsess over it instead of thinking about the one I'd lost.

But five months on, I like you. I've told you, but you say we want different things. You say I want too much – that I am too much. That I need to dial it down a bit. Chill out.

The sex is amazing, and as a person and a friend, he is great. As a man I'm romantically involved with, he makes me feel like I'm not good enough: too fat, too loud, too needy. I end up tired, either from late night sex or wondering why I don't warrant a response to my last text.

There's no middle ground with you. But somehow, I feel like it's all my fault that I can't get it to work. I'm too much.

Maybe that's why they never stay.

BANANA DRAMA

I matched with a guy thirteen years my junior on an app. We messaged back and forth the whole of the first day, then he asked for my Instagram (not my number!). We moved off the app on to Insta DM and the joys of disappearing videos. He had a thing for 'licking'.

I would receive a daily message saying, 'Send me a lick'. After the first few I thought I needed to up the ante. First was an ice lolly and next came a banana... My frazzled brain wasn't thinking straight and the first video I sent was of me licking an UNPEELED banana. It wasn't good. He said to me, 'Why didn't you peel the banana first?' What an idiot! So, I sent a second version of me licking and sucking a peeled banana. At the very end of the video, the banana broke in half and fell on the floor, and I burst out laughing. Not sexy, but he seemed to like it. I felt like a two-bit porn star.

Never again.

FAMILY TENSIONS

When my daughters were at home from school and university over the summer and my husband was working from home every day, I didn't have a moment to myself. The lack of privacy created frustration as I couldn't masturbate. Finally, in September, the girls went back to school and university. Now my husband and I sometimes have sex during his lunch break, which is a bonus as I can be as loud as I want and I'm less sleepy than when we squeeze in a quiet fuck late at night.

IT'S SILLY, SEXY AND I LIKE IT

Out of the blue, an ex-colleague texted me. We have zero in common except our love of the same football team. He is a tough guy – slightly scary but charming. His texts went from 'Long time, how are you?' to 'Let's have drinks', to general chat. Then they plummeted into seriously heart-stopping filthy talk.

He vanished for two weeks. Then he reappeared, resumed the saucy convo and vanished again. This behaviour would normally have no appeal but right now, it's silly, sexy and I like it.

WEIGHTY WORDS

I have spent the last year focusing on self-love and accepting my body for how it is. Before this, I was training every day and was in a very toxic place, health-wise. I promised myself I would no longer shame myself because of how I looked. Last week I slept with a guy for the first time in a year and when we finished, he poked my stomach and made a comment about my belly. I hate the fact that now I've given him the power to make me not want to eat, to want to work out every day, to weigh myself every morning. I guess the truth is he'll never know that every time I'm naked his words scream in my head.

SAFE SEX

I hadn't seen him since last November. I visited him in Paris but had to return to London. He said he would visit but he didn't. My mobile became my go-between. I'd send him messages, pictures and videos and hoped he would respond in kind. He did. Often. We spent days and weeks anticipating every physical act we'd perform when we next met. It was outrageous and totally unrealistic, but it was fun. Truth is, neither of us wants to travel, so we're in stasis. It's good to have a target, an aim, and it's even better when it's unattainable. Frustration and imagined desire are the new safe sex. One day, I hope we'll still have Paris.

BED IN FLAMES

I got divorced from a marriage that, over thirty-two years, was mostly good. Intense loneliness drove me to try online dating. I was terrified that I would never have feelings for anyone besides the husband I lost.

Then I met him online. We were both turning sixty. We both liked cycling. He kissed me on the first date. I wrapped my arms around him and kissed him back. It is the most intense physical connection I have ever felt. He worships my body that is no longer young and firm. A body that has been altered by surgery for breast cancer. He looks at my naked body and I don't try to hide or look away. One night we were lost in each other, and it suddenly occurred to me that I smelt smoke. We looked up and saw the bedside table and a pillow were on fire!

I'll be going back to France in the fall. We are making the most of the time we have.

IT HAPPENS

Shagged my flatmate drunk.

DATING

The start of a relationship is the exciting part. It glitters and pops, your stomach goes up in flames when you see your phone flash with their name. Everything is fresh and in front of you, full of hope and potential. This one could be *The One*. It's sunlight and brunches and coffee and kisses and the reassuring agony of your feelings: *Do they want me? Do they like me as much as I like them? I really want to see them, touch them, fuck them. When can we meet up?*

Dating seems exciting from the outside. It's the fun part that people in long-term relationships romanticise and mourn not experiencing again. Especially if you got together before dating apps: all that choice, all those people in your phone, right there, a swipe away – there's a certain allure.

However, the reality of dating is often a very different story. A common trope of contemporary dating is that, thanks especially to apps, the early stages involve a lot of virtual communication. While technology can facilitate a sense of connection, it's a connection that's not always based on reality. It allows for projection, analysis and social media stalking to fill holes. The screen-watching, internet-investigating, anxiety-exacerbating, conversation-curating and game-playing can be exhausting.

The process of dating – navigating the stage between attraction and being official – can seem like an endless cycle of false starts and when you're in it, you don't know if it will ever end well. There's blue ticks, red flags, self-doubt, second-guessing, holding back – all because of the burns of the past. Unexplained changes of hearts, ghosting. The return to what feels like endless swiping in the dark.

But then there's also the inhale as you set off once more from the darkness – your eyes lit, synapses crackling, one hand reaching out. *This time,* you think, you can see glitter...

THE CATCH

I'm such a catch...

So why can't it ever just be easy?

MESSAGE ALERT

I hate that you have this kind of power over me. I hate that my entire day or mood can be turned around by your message alert. I hate that I've become so reliant on your validation. Unfortunately, though, I love your face. I love your smell. I love the feeling of your arms around me. The way that when I see you, or even just your name on my phone, my heart rate shoots through the roof. I love these new feelings you have evoked in me, changing my perceptions of how sex should be, filling that void I didn't know I had. You've opened my eyes and flipped my world upside down. I don't have an answer to these feelings inside me. Love and feelings are complicated, and I'm feeling frustrated because if I could switch them off then life would be simpler. All I know is I'm sat here waiting for your name to pop up on my phone.

THE ONE %

I've had a love-hate relationship with dating apps in the past. So many disastrous dates and ridiculous stories, yet I've never given up hope.

I re-downloaded Bumble in March after yet another non-starter relationship. I was swiping through profiles and then I saw you. Handsome as hell in your suit, with the biggest grin on your face. I swiped right and hoped that you had too. 'It's A Match'. I was excited but didn't get my hopes up. After all, you have to be realistic about love – there's a 99% chance a date won't happen.

We messaged back and forth for hours on end, swapped numbers, and one week later we had our first 'date' over a WhatsApp video call. I was terrified. We had been getting on so well over messages – what if it wasn't the same when we spoke? Thankfully, talking to you for three hours was so easy and fun. It was meant to be. Every night we video called each other and talked about the most random topics into the early hours of the morning.

When we met for the first time, we went for a walk. It lasted seven hours and we shared our first kiss. It was magical.

Our picnic date by the river was the day I knew. Laid side by side on a blanket looking up at the clouds and pointing out the funny shapes we saw; laughing hysterically at each other, drinking gin and rolling around kissing the hours away. I couldn't wipe the smile off my face for days until we were reunited.

Three months later I still can't get my head around the fact that you are my boyfriend. Last week you told me you loved me, and I nearly cried with happiness. I thought I knew what love was before, but I had no idea until I met you. I am the happiest that I have ever been.

I never believed in 'The One'. I do now (although I have not told you that). I am just praying that my luck doesn't run out and this never ends.

SWIPE, MATCH, DATE, REPEAT

Swipe, match, date, repeat.

When will my love story turn into something more?

WHAT WAS THAT?

We matched on Tinder. It only took five days for us
to meet in real life. Living in a new city, you felt like
home. Six weeks later, you were gone. 'No chemistry',
you said.

So, what was it that we both felt when we were in each
other's arms at 4 a.m. talking about the future?

AT 2 IN THE MORNING

We had been friends for thirty years living across the
world from one another. We normally spent a couple of
weeks together a year, purely platonic, both singletons.
Lockdown came and he rang me at two in the morning
telling me that he didn't want to lose me to the pandemic.
I realized that I didn't want to lose him either. He flew
across the world to me as soon as he could. We are
getting married and I am still gobsmacked, but we don't
want to waste any more time. Such unexpected love is
astonishing.

WEDNESDAY'S GIRL

Reading back through my diaries dating back to 2015,
I've noticed that I have only been in relationships that

never really progressed past the talking stage. Can you really even call them relationships? They're more like situationships. Their feelings for me seemed to change on a day-to-day basis, they were all so hot and cold. They would tell me what our kids would look like on the Monday. By Wednesday, they would tell me they needed space.

Then I met you. I was so sure we would never work out. What would we have to talk about? Would you get bored if we couldn't have sex? We managed to make it work and I fell ridiculously in love with you. We've already done so much together and have so much planned, but something is off. Maybe it's me? Maybe I'm better online than in person? Why do I feel like Wednesday is coming?

HOW TO LOSE A DATE IN SEVEN DAYS

Day 1: Matched.

Day 2: Texted me all day, Netflix party at night and a seven-hour-long phone call.

Day 3: Texted me some more. Threw some sweet nothings in there for good measure.

Day 4: You called me 'baby' – I wondered if we were soulmates.

Day 5: You said you missed me.

Day 6: We couldn't meet up – you felt I had 'a lot going on'.

Day 7: I never heard from you again.

VIBES

We were from the same home town. We'd been connected on Instagram for five years, intermittently liking each other's posts but never really talking. Then, finally, in June, I drunkenly reached out after a party and coaxed you into a FaceTime call. It lasted five hours.

The next night it was six hours. And every call after that got better as we broke down the barriers of communication and awkwardness simultaneously.

We eventually met a week after that, and I was so relieved that the vibe between us was alive in real life. Casually, I brought up the elephant in the room. The fact you had a photo of yourself with a girl on your Instagram posted a few months before we started FaceTiming. You told me she was a mate – I didn't believe you, but I let it go.

Now, five months after we started talking, we've reverted to just two people who follow each other on Instagram. The vibe is still there, but so is your girlfriend.

MAGIC

We spoke for hours. He told me he was into me and wanted to take things slow. Our energy was electric.

And then poof. He disappeared.

PERIOD SEX

You fed me fantasies of amazing, liberating, without-inhibitions sex. I was looking forward to exploring my desires with you and you were willing to give it time.

But, when the time came to meet up, you just wanted to be friends.

Was I too inexperienced? Not bold enough? Or did you just want sex and feared I would get attached? How can you be 'just friends' with someone you wanted to have period sex with? Why was I comfortable with the idea of trying all this with a jerk like you? Why do I still feel that a part of me will always wonder what sex with you could have been like?

DICK

I matched with a guy on Tinder. We met a few times and had a couple of adult sleepovers. He started to get bored and he disappeared, popping back up a couple of times when it suited him, which I eventually tired of. The final time he reappeared, I gave him a TED talk on how women's time is valuable and we're not to be played with. He finally disappeared for good. His excuse all along was that he was finding life too difficult. No pal, it was easy enough when it suited you, don't blame the universe for your disrespectful behaviour. You're just a dick.

ICY

We connected online. We spoke every day. We watched the fireworks together on FaceTime on New Year's Eve.

I couldn't wait to meet you. I wrote stories about how it made me feel.

Well... we met. We made love. And now you're talking about getting married and moving house and suddenly, MY FEET ARE COLD AS FUCK.

MEN

We matched on Tinder in 2017 but never met, then started speaking again online a few years later. You helped me through an emotional rollercoaster of a time and then finally, we met in person.

We spent a passionate night together and cuddled until the morning. I headed home and couldn't keep the smile off my face. You messaged me two days later and said you wanted to see me again.

Three weeks have passed and we haven't seen each other. Every time I suggest a date, you say you're busy or that you'll need to get back to me. You never do. Yesterday I spotted you on Grindr looking for anonymous sex. How could you prefer to sleep with a stranger when I am just down the road?

Back to square one. Men are hard work.

CHANGE OF APPROACH

The last thing I expected was to fall in love. Single and living alone, I'd been off the apps for years and had all but sworn off dating. Something about the transactional nature of modern dating didn't appeal to me; I like to meet people, to get to know them and understand them while forging a connection – I don't work well at high speed. I also hate how quickly people write each other off. But alone at home one night, I thought, what have I got to lose?

Having taken such a long break, I was able to see the mistakes I kept making when it came to searching for a partner, and decided as an experiment to change the things I value in potential matches. It pushed me to be honest with myself and the people I was chatting to about what I wanted. I couldn't be bothered to play games anymore – what was the point?

In a couple of weeks it'll be a year since I met the funniest, kindest and most glorious partner I could ever ask for. I don't know how it happened but I am so thankful every day it did. I'm certain that, without the app, we'd never have crossed paths in the same city.

READY FOR IT

I'm ready for you. Where are you? What is taking you so long? I am beginning to fear that I will miss you when you do arrive, because of all the pain others have caused in the meantime.

WHERE?

Where are all the caring, loyal, trusting, honest men? Is this even a thing anymore? Am I asking for too much, or do good things come to those who wait?

AND JUST LIKE THAT

Life hit me hard, my anxiety was intense, a guy from work became my rock through it all and one thing led to another. It was always casual, but always felt more...

A year later, I'm convinced it's more than casual, it *has* to be. The way we spend time together, the things he says when we're together, the way he looks at me... So, I take the plunge and ask for more, only to be told, 'but we're just casual'.

And just like that, it's all over.

LIFE RUINER

I'm dating this amazing man who happens to be the nicest I've ever met. He compliments me all the time and makes me feel like the only girl in the world. Maybe that's why I'm not that into him.

I was so used to being treated like I was never good enough for you no matter how hard I tried. And now, I'm only attracted to toxic men like you. Thank you for forever ruining my love life.

EMOTIONAL ATTACHMENT

I started speaking to a guy I met online. He's from another city. We spoke over the phone, texted and Zoomed every day for two weeks and it got a bit too hot too fast. He ended up driving through one night. We got on great. Then he backed off, and stupidly, I let him back in.

He said he was looking for a relationship. We saw each other once a week and at weekends for three months. As I let my guard down and thought we had a future, he did a full 180 and said he needed to be with his kids. But the real reason was that he was not over his ex. He still had hate for her, which is really like love. I was so hurt.

Then I found out I was pregnant... well, I'm not anymore. It's been horrific. He has been there through it but I know it's just through guilt, not love, and that breaks my heart. After what's happened, I feel an emotional attachment which is only natural.

But I still hold out hope we will be together and *that's* why I must walk away.

12 HOURS

I started at a new workplace. I'm twenty-six, he was forty-five, charismatic and knowledgeable (but also married with three children). He started pursuing me and it was just meant to be sex. I placed him quite low down on my list of desirable men.

Then something changed; he started calling and asking me to walk his dog with him. He'd hold my hand for the 20-minute walk and then go home to his family. He did it in public – he wanted to be caught – to save him having to tell her about me.

He texted 24/7 about wanting to see me. Told me he was falling in love with me. Wanting reassurance that I loved him too. I didn't.

He left her for me and turned up at my door. I thought, 'Fuck it. I'm lonely and single and here is a man who wants me.' I let him in, into my home and my bed. He brought his suitcase and asked where the laundry basket was for his socks.

I went to work the next morning and we discussed what we'd have for dinner when I returned home. When I got back at 4 p.m., all his things were gone. He texted to say he had gone home.

12 hours I managed to keep a man.

OVER THE INTERNET

I'd worked hard on myself, was in the best place ever mentally, and was happily single. I got talking online to a man from my gym that I'd fancied for a while. He was twenty-five years older than me, so I never thought anything would come from it.

Once we got talking, we couldn't stop. We spoke literally every day for two months, pretty much 24/7. We learned everything about each other; I opened up to him like I never have to anyone before, and we had amazing online sex.

However, I began to realize that our future plans didn't align. He was travelling in another country and didn't know when, or even if, he was going to return here. This started to play on my mind a lot and make me feel down. My head and my heart were telling me different things.

After avoiding it for a few weeks, I finally summoned up the courage to have the conversation with him. I decided that to protect my own feelings, I had to stop talking to him. He tried to persuade me not to, but eventually said he respected my decision and didn't want to hurt me more in the long run because he couldn't promise me anything. We both agreed it was for the best, and said our goodbyes. I told him if he ever decided to come back here, he could message me. It was inexplicably painful.

It's been two days and I miss him desperately; I've never felt so alone, my chest feels heavy. But I've resisted the temptation to message him. I now know that self-care doesn't always feel good. Who knew you could fall in love and get your heart broken over the internet?

IT'S GONNA GET MESSY

I matched with the guy of my absolute DREAMS on Bumble. I invited him over immediately (because I hadn't had sex in quite a while and I couldn't help myself) and he agreed to come. I was so nervous because he was so FIT. Literally one of the most beautiful humans I've ever laid my eyes on.

We ended up having sex a few times that night and it was the BEST I've ever had in my entire life. We talked as well – he was really sweet and had good banter. Since then, I've seen him a few more times; he's very busy with work so it's not as often as I'd like, but every time has been amazing. I get such a rush when I'm with him it's crazy, I've never felt like this before – especially this soon.

He doesn't want anything serious, but I've kinda started to develop feelings for him so I know it's gonna get messy sooner or later...

LIFE SURPRISES US

A year ago, I had to leave London abruptly and return home to Peru. I posted an Instagram story about it on my way to the airport, and this guy who lived back in Peru replied. I had known who he was for a while because we had friends in common, but we had never properly met. (I might also add that I thought he was really cute.)

We began casually texting from time to time over the following months. We both loved rock music and good films. He made me laugh.

I knew nothing real was gonna happen. At some point I was going to return to London and knew I couldn't be in a long-distance relationship. Plus, I felt he was someone that didn't want anything serious. But life always surprises us.

On our first two dates we walked through parks together. We talked. We listened to music. We ate cold pasta from the same plate.

I guess there was no going back when I realized he had become my best friend. He was the person who made me the happiest and who made me the most sure about myself.

We did long distance and continue to do so. It's hard, but we know it's worth it because, after a few months, we get to be with each other again. In the meantime, we each have someone to listen to our everyday, to motivate us, to make us laugh. Someone who waits for you.

I WASN'T EXPECTING THIS

We matched on Hinge. We started talking soon after. (I'm not too fond of the term 'talking' as it felt so much more than just a mutual exchange of words. It was an exchange of emotions, of thoughts, of opinions and more.) We'd call for hours, watching the skies get darker as our hearts got fuller. He became my evening downtime as much as my morning alarm and it took this separation to bring us closer and closer each day.

A July sunset was hazing over the gorge in Bristol. I packed a bag with my speaker, some ciders and a pasta salad. Anxieties aside, I took the deepest breath before walking around the corner to the spot we had decided to meet at. Should I run up to him like I'm reuniting with a long-lost lover, or play it low key and let him find me? Before I even had time to make up my mind, we locked eyes.

Someone who I had built such an image of in my head was just standing there right in front of me. A mental picture had suddenly become a definitive reality. He smelt so much better in flesh form. I ran to him. We hugged. I looked up at him then we hugged again. We smiled and hugged, then after we finished hugging we hugged once more. Each squeeze deepening the reality of the situation – that he was here and he was real – that this was real. The remainder of our first evening together will live forever in my mind, rent free.

How do I condense our summer into a few sentences? It was textbook falling in love.

We spent weekends exploring the city; a city I know so well but made to feel completely new just because he was in it. He opened doors that the world had closed for me, bringing love and curiosity into every creak. How can two people be so similar but still learn so much from each other every day? During the summer we realized that the house he had agreed to rent before we even met was around the corner from my place! I will forever be indebted to the universe for aligning us this way.

Everyone deserves to be loved like this. It's the kind of love that takes many forms, like a gentle hand hold, a belly full of potent laughter or a tender glance across the room that catches you when you least expect it. Trust me, I was not expecting this.

THE WAY I FEEL

I met you online in October, days after receiving my divorce papers and some terrible dating matches. I managed to hide that I was a bit of a mess and was hopeful as you made me laugh and we seemed to click. We are one month on from our first date and it's like I've known you forever.

The way I feel about you scares the shit out of me, but excites me at the same time. You'll never know, but you saved me from crumbling the day we matched. Thank you.

ZERO EXPECTATIONS

We met on Tinder of all places. I joined with zero expectations and hoping for some LOLs at least. It had been the hardest seven weeks of my life. I had lost my aunt – I never got to say goodbye to her and it haunts me. I was so deep in grief that I needed something light to happen.

Your profile came up and I almost swiped left. Not enough humour I thought, a bit too straight-cut for me. But you had such a kind face, so I figured why not? We matched and it turned out you 'super liked' me. You started the convo, we talked for days and agreed to meet on Friday for our first date, a few drinks. I walked up the tube-station stairs to greet you, all hot and sweaty from rushing, and instantly felt at ease from your warm smile. A few drinks turned into shots, a bottle of gin and takeaway pizza at yours.

We kissed and touched intimately and before I knew it, I was in your bed, naked and weeping after amazing sex. In that moment you comforted me, cuddled me like a long-term lover and reassured me that all the sadness I was feeling about my aunt was OK. You told me that she wouldn't have remembered that difficult last conversation I had with her because she knew I loved her. You will never know how those words still bring me such comfort – even though I've told you so many times.

A few drinks turned into 16 hours, which turned into messaging every day, which turned into dating for nine weeks. You saw me at my most vulnerable yet made me feel so safe and secure. How can a stranger understand me so well? I was right about your kind face. I'm hoping those nine weeks of dating turn into more with you, but I haven't quite plucked up the courage to say that yet.

GOLDEN HOUR

I started dating a really old friend. It was odd. I'm a single mother, so I had to really readjust to the situation of having someone around.

It was like permanent golden hour. He was around me a lot and everything was beautiful, glowy and tinted in the perfect shade. Life was lit up differently.

Then, just like golden hour, he disappeared quickly, after I'd spent just a short time taking in his light.

RELATIONSHIP MATERIAL

Thirty-three and had never had a serious relationship. Always wanted one, but was stuck in a perpetual loop of the ones that I didn't want, wanting me, and the ones I wanted, not wanting me.

Until I met him. Ten years my senior, two kids. A lot of baggage, especially for a first relationship. But if that's what love took, I was willing to try. We started with dates, walks in the park. He was kind, honest, funny and cute. He was an adult – funny but steadfast and intellectual – exactly what I needed. In just one month, I felt a comfort and connection I hadn't before.

He was quickly becoming the most important romantic relationship I'd ever had.

But he was looking to settle down, for a step-mother to his children. He decided that wasn't me. I got the usual 'I've really enjoyed my time with you' and 'you're a wonderful person, I just don't see a future'. I've had it so many times: I'm great, but not serious relationship material. I'd love to know where to get that material, because if I've learnt anything over this past year, it's that I'm tired of going it alone. Maybe it's best I didn't start a relationship with a man who would always, understandably, put me second. Or maybe that amount of change would've been just what I needed. Now I'll never know.

ONLINE DATING IN YOUR 50S

I have been a widow from a young age and unexpectedly – since 2009. At the time of the fatal accident my late husband was involved in, my two daughters were very young. I had to put everything aside, including my full-time job as a journalist, and focus on them and their well-being instead.

I saw them through it all: my eldest graduated from university last year with a first and found a job she loves, and my youngest is in her final year. During this time, I didn't date much: just a few here and there where it always became clear they did not want to commit, or needed me to take care of them while they kept chasing other women.

One day, my daughters (who now spend weekends with their boyfriends and bring their boyfriends' boxers home to go in with our laundry) both asked me what I was going to do when they finally moved out. They know that as a highly sociable person, I absolutely don't like being alone, especially at night. They talked me into online dating, as meeting people face to face is a lot harder now than at any time before. Online dating, joining meet-up groups, connecting with people on social networks (including people I used to know and lost touch with) are all things I have done previously and got nowhere with. In fact, after doing them, I felt better off being on my own. There was already enough stress from other sources.

But still, I thought I would give it one last shot. If I was more selective in my choice of sites and the people I connect with, it should be more manageable this time. After some careful research, I settled for a site that looked like it was for professionals like myself.

I wrote my profile and edited it repeatedly until it was perfect, so that men would know that I was not going to waste time on non-serious stuff: I was looking for a serious, lasting, deep and meaningful relationship. It was advised that I attach a photo to my profile for a better response, so I chose one that wasn't too old.

The moment I did, I was bombarded with messages. It felt like flies gathering over food. I felt overwhelmed and took my picture down; if a potential date was interested, I would ask for his email address and send it to him individually. I'm in my late fifties now and I'm not saying that I'm irresistibly beautiful, but I have been told that I'm quite attractive and don't look my age. Well, thank God for small favours, as my late husband used to say.

One guy approached me after he saw my photo and read my profile. He was using a pseudonym and didn't have a profile photo. He requested that we talk on WhatsApp. I wasn't ready to give him my phone number, so I sent him a link to talk via Zoom. We did talk and I discovered things that made me very uncomfortable: he was in the process of getting a divorce, was extremely religious and on the black list of his country of origin for being an activist. He said he worked as a psychiatrist and that's why he couldn't use his real name or put his photo on the site. I thought to myself 'C'est du n'importe quoi': rubbish, nonsense!

Another one, who said he was a dental surgeon, was the complete opposite of the first guy. He wasn't at all religious, but lied about his age to appear younger. He said his two female assistants created a profile for him because 'they didn't want him to be alone' and that he shared his email address with his 'ex'. I didn't realize he was divorced or separated. He kept moving from room to room while we talked on the phone, as if to avoid being caught! When he found out I was a journalist and that I knew people from his community, some of whom were either former colleagues or friends, he ended the conversation abruptly. More bullshit!

Another one, a creative director, asked why I didn't have a profile picture. I replied that I was happy to email him one after asking a few questions about his marital status. He just vanished.

Another one sent a few messages that I interacted with. Then sent his number and asked that I call him. I thanked him and said I needed to find out a bit more about him first – he kept exaggerating his professional status and making up stories. He got angry (it showed in his language), then kept checking my profile on LinkedIn. I put him in his place and he went quiet.

Am I missing something about men, even at this age? Is it something about online dating and social networks that allows for playing games, lying and taking advantage? I'm not cancelling my membership yet because I paid for six months upfront but, more importantly, because I'm an optimist and I believe that there are still good people out there.

I'M NOT YOUR GIRLFRIEND

I started seeing a guy in June. He was fun, he had a car and he was older. It was a change from the usual skater boys who are really into sound art and bringing down the patriarchy. This guy felt different. He loved football, like really loved it. At first I thought it was good he had a passion, but now, looking back, it should have been a warning sign. Alas, we carried on seeing each other for eight months.

One Friday I had a moment of realisation. I'm not his girlfriend. He's not my boyfriend. Why am I putting up with his shit? I am expecting him to change but he isn't going to and I am not going to either. This isn't anything more than just the option of having someone to spend time with without the commitment of an actual relationship. It was the classic situation of me being obsessed with the person I had created in my head, not actually him.

So, I ended things. It surprised him, and if I'm honest, I surprised myself. For the first time in my adult love-life, I put myself first.

This story is a homage to myself and not ignoring the voice inside my head. I deserve better and I am way fucking better on my own. Something I realized while lying in bed the other night was that I am not dimming my sparkle for anyone, let alone a guy I met off Hinge who still brings his dirty laundry home to his mom.

PIGGY IN THE MIDDLE

We went to school together and bumped into each other at the local pub and reminisced. I woke up beside you the next morning to discover you were still with your long-term girlfriend. I felt awful, but you continued to message me that week asking to see me again and cook me dinner. I said no.

You rang me at the end of the week to say that you had ended it with her; it had been wrong for a long time. You asked again to cook me dinner, so I thought, why not. We have always been flirty friends, and so we slept together.

Fast-forward six weeks, we've been on dates and had adult sleepovers. You told me you had strong feelings for me, that I was your best friend. That I was your favourite person. That maybe we should call it off in case you fuck up and hurt me. I told you to get a grip, man up and just enjoy whatever our situation is.

Fast forward to today. I have discovered you never broke up with her. You've just signed a mortgage together. I realize you are a pig.

SUPERMARKET SWEEP

I was ghosted by three men I was barely interested in and groped by a man while shopping for groceries.

IRL

I matched with this god of a man on Hinge. He was gorgeously fit. We started FaceTiming every night. Not only was he fit, but he was also a dream. Kind, funny, loved his family, loved the outdoors, loved his job. He's in the army, so basically a proper hunk.

As time went on, I suppose it felt like we really knew each other. After all, we had been in touch most days on video call. He came to London to see me (he's from up North and didn't quite understand the importance of setting your distance parameters on Hinge). We set off for the pub (I'd had a few prior. Dutch courage and all).

We had nothing to say to one another all night. The chat was dead, sparse, zero, nada. No chemistry, no conversation, nothing. I will never know how FaceTime tricked me so badly, but all I can say is that

I will be a little more careful next time. Anyhoo, the search continues...

BUSY

I'd been single for a year after my relationship with my ex ended and honestly had the best time just being with me, but I thought I'd better make an effort and see what was out there. A few weeks ago, I meet with this guy. To be honest, he didn't much look like his profile but it was my first date in a year, so I went along with it just to get out the house.

He was actually really lovely. We swapped numbers and went out again for dinner. No cheeky kiss afterwards – just a hug, but I'm OK with that. On to date three. He comes to my house for dinner. It was great. We chatted, drank wine, stayed up late and he stayed over. Nothing happened except a kiss and cuddle.

Two weeks later (yes, a whole two weeks) and we're on to date four. He was picking me up. I said he could stay over if he wanted a drink. He said yes. So he pulls up outside my house. I wait for him to knock. He's a while sitting in the car so I thought he must be on the phone. Ten minutes later I check. He's left!

I casually message to ask if he was OK and got a blunt, 'busy atm' reply. Odd. He then cancels 10 minutes later as 'something has come up'. And that was the last I heard from him. That was a week ago.

I know I deserve better, but it was nice to think this could have gone somewhere. The worst part is

I had nothing in for dinner, so I had to have a beige freezer tea.

(NOT QUITE) A YEAR IN DATES

Let's take it month by month.

January: Just broke up with my ex, 'Bar Bob'. Heartbroken. Was a dramatic movie-esque whirlwind romance with an equally dramatic end. Boy meets girl in bar. Boy hands girl business card. Boy and girl fall in love and then do two months long distance while girl travels the world having just quit her job to go and 'find herself'. Boy is shit at communicating. Boy and girl reunited. Boy messes things up, they break up on New Year's Eve – how romantic.

February: Feeling lonely. Valentine's Day sucks. Reach out to ex for a night of feeling less lonely. Short term, a great idea. Long term, a terrible idea. Back to being lonely.

March: Time to hit the dating apps. Match with cute guy (let's call him Tinder Tom) just before I flee the Big Smoke for a wholesome three months with my sister, niece and nephew in the countryside.

April–May: Beginning of a long-distance, Dickensian-esque romance (with phone calls instead of love letters and Zoom dates instead of bareback riding through fields of wheat). Very wholesome, maybe virtual dating is the way forward?

June: Move back to London. Get to meet Tom. Things start off well, until he invites me round. His flat is a state. Dirty. Messy. Stinks of weed. He didn't even put clean sheets on the bed. Turns out there's a reason virtual dating works. Note to self, next time ask for a virtual tour of their flat on the first date. Onwards and upwards.

July–August: Back on the apps. Meet a new, even cuter guy. Let's call him Hinge Harry. We have a few great dates. Things are going well. That is, until, I get carried away in the moment and declare my undying love for him. Insert face-palm emoji. He panics. Tells me he isn't over his ex of eight years and isn't ready for another relationship, nor is he any good at casual flings. Erm, so what exactly are you doing on a dating app, Harry? Back to being lonely and heartbroken. Back to hours of endless horizontal thumb exercise.

September: A series of terrible decisions and car-crash dates. 1. Reached out to a cute guy from way back in my uni days. Turns out there was a reason it didn't work out back then. Some things are better left in the past. 2. Couple of dates with someone off an app. Going reasonably well, until I got the ick mid-sex. To which my therapist's response was 'maybe let's avoid sleeping with people until at least the third date?' Insert second face-palm emoji. The list goes on, but I'll spare you the gory details.

October: A few dates with a friend of a friend who was genuinely lovely, really cared about me and treated me really well. Turns out there is such a thing as 'too nice' and I decided that we were better as 'friends'. Back to the apps. A few more dates. Turns out when you stop caring and stop looking for anything serious, you actually have more fun. And so far, my therapist would be proud.

What an emotional rollercoaster of a year.

NO EXCUSE

We met online. After a couple of phone calls, we had lunch and later a romantic dinner, after which we kissed. We'd speak a couple of times a week and meet on weekends. The last time we met I went as her plus-one to a July 4th BBQ. It was fun. My mistake was not calling her the following week. I just didn't. No excuse. This was her last text:

'As I haven't heard from you since the party last Saturday, I assume you did not have a good time and we have come to the end of the road. Wishing you all the best.'

BARE MINIMUM

I met someone online and had my first long-distance relationship. I really thought we clicked, and I enjoyed being on calls with him at night as well as texting him. We had been talking for almost a month and, I regret what I'm about to say, but he asked for some nudes. I trusted him so I sent some.

After that day, I didn't hear from him for a whole three weeks, throughout which I had been sending him messages every once in a while. I got nothing – not even a read message. I sort of got fed up and guessed I got ghosted, so I sent my last message to cut ties.

I never did hear back from him.

CONNECTING

I watch you laugh through the poorly connected WiFi and think...

Fuck. We have a connection.

ON A WHIM

I wasn't looking for anything serious; I struggle to let people in and to commit. We had matched and exchanged a few messages, but I wasn't really that interested. I asked if he was free one evening, on a whim, and we clicked like I have never clicked with anyone before. Our date almost outran the trains, and we soon became inseparable.

If we aren't together we're texting or calling. I always thought it was bullshit that the whole world could disappear when you're with *that* person, but it happened. He has broken down my barriers and melted my icy core. We've hit bumps along the way, which have thankfully only made us stronger. Now we are in a relationship, and it is worth every second. Not bad for two commitment-phobes. Now I'm working up the courage to tell him I love him.

HANDSOME VIKING

I was thirty and had been single for years with most of my friends married or in relationships. I never had much luck online dating, meeting commitment-phobic and often not-very-nice men. I carried on dating, refusing to settle as a cat lady – there was surely someone lovely out there for me.

I came across this handsome Viking on Hinge. He had great chat and we had plenty in common; we're both twins, the same age and a shared love for spicy margaritas. We met for our first date in May, sipping on gins in tins, flirting in the park until dark. The weeks followed with endless alfresco dining on my patio soaking up the summer sun, and passionate nights in. I'd never felt happier that I could meet someone like him – a kind, hilarious, true gentleman (who had an insane body – ooof!). I had this new feeling that I couldn't explain. A few weeks in I told him I loved him, and he said it back.

He moved into mine in November and threw me the best thirty-first birthday party. I can't imagine what life would be without him. I met my soulmate. He was worth the wait.

BEFORE THE FIRST DATE

We had liked each other before, but circumstances weren't right. We reconnected in February – texting, chatting, getting excited about one another and the potential of this new thing. Made plans to meet but something came up, made new plans but fell ill. We text every day, good morning to good night. Phone calls and video calls. But haven't kissed, touched one another, been in the same room. The initial lust and excitement – 'I can't wait to see him. I NEED to see him.' – gave way to a reassuring security – knowing he was there for me, and I was there for him – gave way to a nagging disappointment – is he always this negative? He puts so much pressure on me. He complains constantly. This is exhausting.

Have I run the gamut of an entire relationship without even one date? One kiss?

I WANT IT ALL

I want dusty museums, musicals in the West End, gritty theatre in Brixton and drag shows in Camden. I want galleries, trains, gigs and laughs. I want plans to cancel and nights I forget.

I want to stick to the floor of a cheap bar and pay too much money for a G&T in Soho.

I want drunk texts, late-night Ubers across town, wine in a garden in Wandsworth, fighting off squirrels and hay fever.

And I want it all with you.

A WOMAN'S INTUITION

I knew after our first exchange of messages that you were going to break my heart. I knew it was going to end in tears. There were no red flags, the conversation was smooth, you asked questions, there was chemistry. And yet there were subtleties that something wasn't right.

If only there was a way for a woman's intuition to be packaged and sold.

As I walked towards you sitting on the bench, I took a deep breath in. The way you'd nonchalantly hung your foot over your knee and glanced down at your phone gave me high-school butterflies. I hadn't felt them in years, and that was all it took!

You glanced upwards as I approached and stood without rushing, not a nerve in sight, and walked calmly towards me. 'Hi. How are you?' I could hear your smile as you spoke, it spread to your gorgeous green eyes, too.

We walked along the pier and sat down on some rocks that placed us close together, but not close enough to touch. I fought the urge to slip my arms around your waist and pull you towards me. As we looked out to the sea and the setting sun behind the city, my favourite dusty pink haze was beginning to form on the horizon. 'It's funny,' I said, as I looked at your handsome, bearded, olive-skinned face, 'I told my sister earlier that I was meeting a guy on the beach at sunset and we laughed at how this is an especially romantic first date.' You smiled and winked, and I melted. Part of me wanted to get up and leave at that very moment. I was terrified at the thought of what was coming, yet already completely addicted to you. We clinked our bottles, 'Here's to meeting strangers at the beach for beers.'

It's such an odd phenomenon to meet a new person and instantly connect with them. I know it happens, but really, *how* does it happen? Two people from different cultures, finding a shared humour, finishing each other's sentences. I couldn't take my eyes off your pillow lips and perfect white teeth. The way you gently threw your head back as you laughed made my stomach flip. I wanted to swallow you up whole! Those long, dark eyelashes. What must it feel like to be as quietly self-confident as you are, but with an ego so thoroughly in check? To glide through life drawing people in. What's that personality type? A Campaigner. Oh, my Lord, that smile. You were just so fucking cool.

The next three hours were dreamlike. We danced around each other as we wandered the streets, laughing – so much laughing! – flirting, fire touches every now and then. We joked about drinking on park benches, making us feel like rebellious teenagers stealing precious time together in a world of rules and forbidden love. Eventually, we settled in a square and you leant in close. I was finally going to taste those pillow lips...

To say I hadn't experienced a perfect first kiss before I kissed you is not an exaggeration. With every gentle move, I felt lightning travel from my mouth to my toes. The pace quickened slightly and the urgency increased.

'We absolutely cannot go back to mine. My flat is a fucking tip, I was not expecting this,' I giggled as I dragged you directly towards my flat. You grabbed me and pulled me into a doorway. We were acting like teenagers again, with our hands gliding everywhere. Our breaths short, lips on lips, lips on necks.

The instant connection translated to bed. To be able to communicate so freely with someone new, have them listen and understand you, was magic. But my favourite thing was how we laughed. So much laughter and fun amongst all the passion. My face hurt from smiling.

And then we lay in comfortable silence next to each other, staring up at the ceiling. No contrived hugging, no awkward spooning, just pure, intimate ease. Like we'd done this a million times before. But soon came your 'I have to go'; curfew was approaching.

We dressed in silence. The kiss at my door was achingly tender, I felt like I was going to cry. You cupped my left cheek with your right hand, your pillow lips lingered three seconds longer than was needed. 'I'll text you,' you said but we both knew you wouldn't.

The second you left the stomach churn started. I took two sleeping pills just to get through the night. In the morning I immediately got to work with the new information I had gleaned, letting my gut lead the way to feed the gnawing.

It didn't take long, the world we live in now is scary.

Your full name...
Your LinkedIn...
Your Facebook...
Your profile picture...
Her name...
Her Instagram...
... You're married.
I'm a mess.

IT'S
COMPLICATED

The hardest relationships to process are usually the
ones that we don't have a suitable term for. The
ones that fall outside our vocabulary and live out
in the wilderness of unclear relationship status, in
which feelings can be invalidated, ignored, confused,
misconstrued and abused. The long-term, agonizing
head fuck.

The not-quite-official.
The long-term affair.
The not-just-friends-but-not-having-sex-either.
The is-this-really-just-sex?

These relationships always seem so clear to call
from the outside. But jump inside them and you'll
drown in the messy soup of maybes and giving a
fuck. Inside these relationships, the jaggedy nuances
of knowing that the other person is also a complex
human being fractures any clarity. You'll tie yourself
in knots, getting lost analysing the minute details,
using your intimate knowledge of yourself and the
other person - and your empathy - to create a web
of explanations around the situation. Any reason to
hope will justify hanging in there for just a little bit
longer. Often, these relationships come with the
internalised shame of feeling that we shouldn't be in
them. Which is unhelpful because we are. Sometimes

we get ourselves into situations that aren't ideal, that are messy. We're human.

Even at the best of times, people are complicated, and so are relationships. Some people get under our skin, and we go along for the ride rather than walking away and wondering 'what if?'. Sometimes we don't realize what we've walked into until we're too far in to find our way back out. These relationships don't happen with people you feel ambivalent about. These people make you feel ultra-alive. Around them, you're star-like. So bright, you're burning. Do you even want to be put out?

STATEMENTS

It had been a year since we last spoke, a year since my friend held my hand in the police station as they wrote down my statement. And now we're seeing each other again as if nothing happened, spending endless days and nights kissing, talking, cooking. You make me so happy in these little moments, but in the back of my mind I know it's not going to last – it never does with you. I can't tell you, but the guilt of keeping our secret is eating me up inside. No one knows, not my friends, not my family. Everyone still thinks I have your number blocked in my phone.

WOMEN

I'm a married woman. I've been married to a man for twenty years. I have children. This year, I fell in love with a woman. I have had to face some hard truths about accepting this part of myself that I've hidden all my life. It's been the scariest, most painful thing I've ever done. My journey is not over and I have a long way to go. I don't know what the ending of my story will look like yet.

MY EX'S OLD LOVER

I call my ex's old lover during lockdown. Late at night, after a bottle of wine. It's been over three years but it still hurts like hell. 'Caller, do you want to talk?' she asks. But I can't bring myself to say the words. To ask her why she broke my heart, dismantled our family. And now he's moved on. I hear her TV in the background and it comforts me to think that she is also alone, the two of us, united by our pain.

DARK

For years you were my world and you hurt me every day. Every time you cheated I forgave you, but I couldn't forget. You broke me.

He has built me back up and helped me recover. He is sweet and kind and we laugh at each other's silly jokes. He moved in and we are spending every minute together.

Last night it was dark when we were having sex. I couldn't see his face. But in my mind, I saw yours.

I miss all the heartache you gave me.

DO I KEEP WAITING FOR HIM?

I'm in love with a guy that I've been talking to on and off for four years now. I've believed for most of that time that we were moving towards something more serious. But he's recently said he is still not ready, hates talking about it, and it'll be six months before he'll know what he wants from me and his life.

Obviously, I don't want to pressure him, as it's understandable to be uncertain. But I can't help it, I just want to be his everything. I want to do normal relationship things, have dinner, stay over, go on days out, but all we do is message and sext. He says he likes me a lot, and could want something with me in the future, but doesn't want to discuss it because it stresses him out.

I haven't seen him for eight months because he won't tell his family about me for religious reasons and is always busy. I've said no to meeting up just for sex because I'm serious about wanting more. I still don't know if that was the right decision. Recently I downloaded the dating apps because I wanted to make him jealous – but now I'm at odds. Should I try to move on? Or do I wait for what could be something great? I really want it to be with him, but I don't know when he will be ready. It'll break me if it doesn't work out.

TIMING

By this time next week, you will be here.

It's been thirteen years, four countries, one night spent in your bed, one night with you in mine – oh and that one time on my couch – a couple of drunken kisses, countless exes and even more lovers, since we met at university.

You were a year ahead, with such kind eyes and a deep laugh – I was instantly smitten. We always had good chemistry, the conversation was easy and flirting came naturally. But I was always dating someone else. We finally hooked up two years later, and it was so much better and more than I thought it would be. A few days later I asked you out, but you turned me down. A relationship wasn't what you wanted. Timing wasn't right. I like to think that on some level, you always knew that I was more than a casual relationship. We had another drunken hook-up on my couch, a couple of months later, which again left my head swimming.

A few months after that night, you asked me out, but I'd started dating someone new a couple of weeks before. It seemed the timing was always wrong. I ended up staying with him for six years. I was good and faithful to him... except that one very drunken night you and I made out after dancing at a friend's birthday party. And that night a few years later, before you moved away when you hugged me like the world was ending and pinned me up against the wall outside the bar, and we very nearly went back to my place, before your friend came back and I came to my senses. And that Sunday when you were in town, when I lied about who I was having brunch with, and we walked around our university campus, and kissed in the quad, so intensely that my head spun, reigniting passion that I hadn't felt in years. I broke up with my ex five days later.

Two weeks after that, when things were less complicated, we had that magical, passionate afternoon in my bed. Fuelled by reignited passion and the intensity of knowing this was only a tiny stolen moment in time, the world stood still for a couple of hours. You had to move to Japan a couple of weeks later. The timing was still wrong.

We last saw each other nearly two years ago. I was about to move here, and you had just found out that you'd be moving here in two years' time. I had a wretched break-up, and you were trying to make long distance work with someone halfway around the globe from you. You still hugged me close and held me like the world was ending. Maybe timing would never be right.

We've stayed in touch, more so than ever before. Despite being in different countries and time zones, we've gotten closer than ever. We text all the time, have even started video chatting. I thought at first it was just friendly, that only I was starting to have feelings, but between the birthday present, and the video chatting, and the flirty texting that not infrequently turns into innuendoes, it has gotten harder to deny that you aren't feeling the same. You move here next week. And maybe after thirteen years, maybe, for the first time ever, our timing is right?

TEN THINGS I HATE ABOUT YOU

1) I hate your bad grammar.
2) I hate how opinionated you are.
3) I hate that you haven't wanted to reach out to me.
4) I hate that the fact you haven't means you're a better person than if you had done.
5) I hate that my mind hasn't caught up with my actions yet to move on.
6) I hate that I still miss you – it's quite frankly not normal how much I do.
7) I hate that I have a hunch you feel the same, even if you've suppressed it better than I have. You're like the north magnet to my south, and ignoring that pull is exhausting.

8) I hate that I can't say any of this to your face.
9) I hate that you lied to me.
10) I hate that you met her first.

IF YOU'RE WONDERING

If you're wondering if I ever loved you, I did.

I still do.

WHAT IF?

I went travelling with my best friend and fell in love with her along the way. We'd been best friends for years but always felt more than just a friendship, we'd always hinted our bi-curiosity and eventually ended up secretly getting together whilst travelling. Eventually, we had to come home. After spending every day, and every hour, with her it was difficult being apart. We missed each other so much. During the first couple of weeks we spoke everyday, but it took time to decide whether we wanted a relationship or not – it could ruin our friendship in the long run.

We spent weeks being weird around each other, not knowing how to be just friends around each other. She soon ended up getting with a new guy in our friendship group and I spent every gathering having to watch them together. It's not easy seeing that.

We're still good friends and gradually getting over the love interest, but I always wonder what might've happened.

PLAYING WITH FIRE

He is a best friend and a confidant. He is an ear every morning and evening. He is the person I want to speak to before I go to sleep. He is caring, charming, charismatic and confident. He is passionate, playful and patient. But importantly he is married.

I know I'm playing with fire.

HOLDING HANDS IN MELBOURNE

We started as new friends getting to know each other during long walks. Then we spent three weeks sleeping together. I think we both felt like it had the potential to be very serious.

But now we've spent two months apart. While neither of us is fucking anyone else, you still 'aren't sure if you're ready for a new relationship', so we're keeping our distance.

I wish you'd just tell me what I want to hear. That you do want a relationship. Because I know I do. You say everything else that I want to hear, except that. And then I feel guilty and pathetic for thinking that way.

So we're back to going for walks together. But these days we hold hands.

And I found myself thinking about that blind Dutch man who broke my heart last year, who wouldn't hold my hand because he'd 'been that man' for his ex and he wasn't going to 'be that man' again. And I think of you and your ex, who you still mention often, and I'm just waiting for you to turn around and say the same thing, and drop my hand.

QUEEN OF HEARTS

Last night I put my cards on the table.

Last night you told me you weren't over your ex.

Last night I found my self-respect and wished you well.

BULLETS

Six years ago, you told me you had feelings for me and I shot you down. I was in a relationship. I was happy.

Six years on, in the same relationship, I watch you with her – exploring the world, buying a house and getting married – wondering what could've been.

You're the one that got away.

It should've been me.

WHAT I'VE TRIED

This is madness. It was well over a year ago. And I have tried everything:

I've tried reaching out

I've tried giving you space

I've tried focusing on myself

I've tried a gratitude journal

I've tried singing ABBA every time you pop into my brain

I've tried putting my energy into my career

I've tried new hobbies

I've tried new people

I've tried blind dates

I've tried letting my friends set me up

I've tried every single (exhausting) dating app

I've tried meeting someone just like you

I've tried dating your polar opposite

I've tried seeking a new love of my life

I've tried casual sex

I've tried dating three guys at the same time

I've tried dating girls

I've tried going on so many dates

I've tried focusing on self-love

I've tried practising gratitude to the loving relationships
with my family and friends

I've tried getting drunk

I've tried to make peace

I've tried cursing you

I've tried ranting about you to my friends

I've tried to be your friend

I've tried blocking you

I've tried over-analysing every interaction

I've tried giving you the silent treatment

I've tried to make peace with your lack of feelings

I've tried hyping myself up

I've tried grounding myself

I've tried meditation

I've tried yoga

I've tried self-help books

I've tried loving myself

I've tried comfort eating and control eating

I've tried buying a whole load of sex toys

I've tried being keen
I've tried being nonchalant
I've tried never listening to our soundtrack ever again
I've tried to accept that you have a new girlfriend
I've tried to accept your lack of feelings towards me
I've tried everything.

I don't what else to do. Even at my best, I miss you. I think I might love you. I wish you'd come back into my life. I think you might be my soulmate.

TANGLED WEB

It was the kind of sex that makes others suck the air between their teeth and say, 'It'll never last'. No one's presence has ever made as much sense to me as yours, even though we make no sense. But it didn't last, of course.

You called and texted from the spare bedroom every night, not knowing your wife was pregnant in the next room. I never told you that my sister was born into a similar situation. I wish I could tell you how that played out.

I really do hope you'll be the best fucking dad to that kid. But I can't help but wonder, is she only with you for financial security? Did she really not notice the scratch on your neck?

LIMBO

We met at university in February. He wore black, thick-rimmed glasses, and in our very first conversation we bonded over a mutual love for the same local pub. As the weeks progressed, we'd linger on street corners after class to chat and chat and chat. We'd find any excuse to start a texting conversation. We spent Friday nights in the library together finishing off our assignments. We had rooftop pints and admired a rainbow. He met my housemates. I met his brother. But was it just friends?

We'd text throughout our classes. And we'd go for walks together after. Long walks, and he'd constantly astonish me with the same interests or ideas. We started a list of things to do featuring movies and places we wanted to share with each other. Surely, this wasn't just friends?

We got drunk at his house. One thing led to another. He rocked up unannounced to my house with homemade brownies when I said I was stressed.

And then our clashing insecurities surfaced. His fear of entering a relationship again. My fear of rejection. I became snappy on the phone. Argumentative. Frustrated. Unpleasant.

It felt like it was time to end things. Give up. I decided that he didn't want me, like I wanted him. So, we met up for a walk. It was awkward, at first. We sat on a bench, and I didn't think it was possible for his body to press any further away from me. But we talked. And laughed. And talked over the top of each other. In a good way. It felt normal again.

And so we're back to normal and will just have to see what happens.

Sorry that's such a cliffhanger to end on, but I guess for now we're in limbo.

THE TERRIBLE THING

I miss you quite terribly.

But I know, I need to leave you alone.

HARD

I stood in your bedroom this morning about to say goodbye. I was in last night's dress, a long floaty flowery number from the back of my wardrobe. I hadn't seen you for nearly a year. My letters from the last two years were in a small pile underneath your table, all within reach, with indications that they'd been read more than once.

I slept on the sofa last night as it became the least comfy but most graceful option. I had intended to finally give myself to you, but after we'd had the 'talk', while you were in the shower, I realized that I would rather die a virgin than give myself to someone who didn't know my worth.

We should stay only friends you said, you didn't want to lose the emotional support or the beautiful friendship we had. I would be 'convenient and comfortable' for you in a relationship, and you didn't want that.

We're both moving to the same city, finally near one another, just a month apart. However, you said wanted to explore the city alone.

You have two exes in the same city who you still call regularly; is it one of them you'd rather be with?

I am relieved you were honest. I have embraced the heartache and stupidity I had. I was naive to think that the gifts you gave me, the late-night phone calls, the lengthy messages from you meant something else.

So why is it when I stand in your room to say goodbye, your response isn't just one of friendship – those bedsheets don't hide you being hard. What's worse is the goofy shy smile on your face while it happens, not hiding the fact by saying it was 'spectacular' to see me.

God, I'm so frustrated and you're a dick. Why does that make me want you even more?

REMINDERS

I remind myself he's an arse and I should not go back. I tell myself: look at how he treated you:

1. He doesn't want to touch you.
2. He doesn't want to kiss you.
3. He doesn't want to have sex with you.
4. He doesn't talk to you.
5. He doesn't reply to you – or even read your messages. He doesn't answer the phone!
6. He doesn't want to see you.
7. You are at the bottom of his priority list.

8. He stands you up.
9. He's ashamed of you. Hasn't introduced you to friends/family.
10. He didn't make an effort to cook or clean.
11. He never acknowledged any of the gifts you bought him.
12. He's there for her and her family.
13. He said you annoy him, pressure and hassle him.
14. He doesn't wish you luck/ask how your day was.
15. He doesn't come home for dinner when he's supposed to.

LOCKDOWN BROUGHT ME BACK MY BEST FRIEND

In July 2013 I went on holiday with my mum to Turkey. My mum and I would go out for dinner and come back to the hotel bar for drinks. One evening, back at the hotel, we started talking to this family. This is where I met him. We would talk for hours, drink cocktails and sneakily have a cigarette behind our parents' back. As we got to know each other, we realized we lived in neighbouring villages back home. After that first night, it became a routine that, as families, we would go out for dinner and drinks.

He and his family left Turkey before us, so we did the usual Facebook add and said we would stay in touch. The next day, I had a Facebook message from him saying it was lovely to meet and we should stay in touch. We did, and we became the best of friends.

We ended up applying and both getting in to the same university. So excited to be in the same city together, we spoke all the time and planned our first year as students. We both got dropped off at university and started freshers' week. On our first night out, we drunkenly kissed, but never spoke about it. Over first year, we spent more time together; went out all the time and would go back to his family's house for Sunday lunch and home comforts from time to time. At the summer ball at the end of first year, I had a lot to drink and told him I had feelings for him. He said he felt the same. The next morning, I woke up in a panic and ignored his messages. I went home for summer and continued to ignore him.

We lost touch, went on with our lives and our studies. He removed me from everything, but I still had his family on Facebook, so would see where he was in life.

A few years went by. I had always regretted how I dealt with the situation, running away just because I was scared of how I felt. I messaged him on Facebook and apologised, said I was wrong to treat him like that, and he hadn't deserved that. I didn't expect a response, I just wanted to tell him how truly sorry I was. A few days later, he replied thanking me for the apology, but said he didn't want to rekindle any form of communication or friendship. I understood and didn't press further.

A year passed and out of the blue, he messaged me, saying that he had been looking through old pictures and that he was sorry for having been blunt before, he was just surprised to hear from me. We messaged back and forth for a bit – but that was it.

In the summer of lockdown, I was on Instagram and came across his profile. I decided to follow him, and he followed me back. He messaged me and we spoke on the phone a few times. We were both going through tough times and tried to help each other out. In December, it was his birthday. We went out for drinks and dinner, and I felt exactly the same as I did when I was nineteen at the summer ball. But this time I was twenty-five and not scared, just safe and happy. When I left, he said, 'Don't be a stranger this time.'

There hasn't been a day since that we haven't spoken. We have openly spoken about things and haven't hidden our feelings like we did all those years ago. We spent NYE together and, although I am based in London and he's in Bristol, we want to see what happens. I don't know where this is going, but I have never been this happy and can't wait to see what the future holds.

HEY GOOGLE

When I got so drunk that I started telling you everything I like about you, words came easy then.

I almost told you that night when I said I had a crush on someone.

I almost told you again when we were done for the night and I wrote out the longest message in my iPhone.

Then I woke up, and erased it.

What were you going to say that night when you didn't finish your sentence?

Why can't I just get this out?

Even worse, why can't I just stop feeling this way?

Hey Google, how do you unbreak your own heart?

PENDULOUS

I. Swinging Forward

I thought I was being brave. I remember most of my
friends asking me to be careful and cautious – to ensure
that I protect my sensitive heart when I discussed my
situation with them. While I love them for seeing the
big picture and being excellent advisors, I do wish they
weren't so right.

II. Swinging Backward

I went into it thinking I have a grip on my feelings,
that I don't feel anything for him: 'I'm not sure he is
my type. Besides he has a girlfriend. So what if we met
on a dating app and he is in an open relationship?
We are keeping things non-sexual, this is my boundary
and I can maintain it. If he oversteps, I'll tell him.
He seems really sensitive and empathetic, so I'm sure
he would listen. I am certain I need/want a long-term
monogamous partnership, so this is not for me. This is
just companionship, a platonic relationship of sorts. I
don't know what type of person I am looking for anyway,
so I would come out of this learning more about myself, a
worthy experiment of sorts. No?'

III. Swinging Forward

During a few months of constant daily chats spanning the mundane as well as the political, gallery hopping, discussing Beardsley's style and the ideals of masculinity, a few weekend trips where we savoured the landscapes, food and each other, I fell for him so bad. Unfortunately, he was everything I was looking for – the one who saw me, heard me and made me feel safe – but the one I couldn't have. Gosh! How had I let this happen?!

IV. Swinging Backward

His girlfriend was due to come back a bit before the end of the year, as her overseas contract was reaching its end. With the uncertainty of the pandemic, there was no clarity around what would happen next: if her employers would extend her contract or not, whether she would be able to travel back or not. If she would choose to stay or not. She definitely wanted to live abroad. He, however, did not want to move. London is where he saw his life to be. He supported her decision but didn't like the situation in which he found himself. He was unable to meet her regularly, as they had originally planned. He just wanted his girlfriend back with him.

The open relationship was a necessary compromise so they could both meet other people and not feel lonely. One she had asked for, and the reason they were both on a dating platform. She was already seeing someone when we met. He wasn't. He said it gave him the opportunity to meet new people and he was only looking to make new friends in the city. The dating platform made sense as they had allowed each other to have sexual experiences if they wanted. Things do get lonely, he said. It all seemed like a very pragmatic decision, but I got the sense of something else brewing beneath. I wasn't completely sure they had their open relationship dynamic sorted, or had really discussed their feelings at length. There seemed to be more than what was being expressed. I didn't probe more or ask what her end of the deal was. We were just friends at the time.

As time went on and we spent more time together, we decided to date until she got back. I started to care a lot about him. Things quickly got more complicated and confusing as new conditions started to emerge. She did not want me to be a part of their life if/when she got back. But he wanted me in his, as a friend at least, if not more. She had enough friends and didn't need more, was her claim. He maintained that he didn't and was one of the major factors for opening his relationship. He asked me to be in his life and seemed to think I would definitely be a part of some future he was imagining. How was that even possible? Did he want to keep fighting her so he could spend time with me? And how could we be friends/acquaintances after all that we had been through and I had fallen for him?

He did ask me to wait for him at one point, probably in one of those moments of passion. I won't deny that a part of me felt great, since he was hinting that he had made a choice of sorts. But I was never really certain of what he wanted, and neither was he. When I asked him what he meant a few days later, he felt confused. Even if I wasn't sure what I was looking for, his confusion and ambivalence were definitely not appealing. Further, if he did choose to be with me, would that ever feel fulfilling? Destroy what they built for four years over the less than four months we had spent together? And was I really *that* sure about him?

I decided that I'd had enough and asked that we break up. He took a few days to think about it and said it made sense. He had a lot that he had built with her – friends, family, relationships – and it would be a shame to lose it all. I won't deny that those words really, really hurt.

He wished I could still be his friend or would at least keep in touch with him periodically, but I really couldn't. I completely cut him out of my life. I was feeling anxious and jealous while I was supposed to just have fun and experiment. And just like that, in only a few months, we went from being companions, to lovers, to strangers.

V. Swinging Forward

I do think I was brave in choosing myself when the situation demanded. Whether it was a worthy experiment is probably too soon to say. I have been processing it all over the last two months and continue to. I have also signed up for therapy. The loss has definitely shattered my heart. I can't believe that I met someone when I wasn't actively looking for anyone and ended up liking them. (I haven't properly dated in the last eight years. I've had an occasional hook-up or fling but nothing more. Ha! Life.)

My emotions swing like a pendulum. I miss him a lot and wish things could be like they were in summer, or that I could just write to him. But then I ask myself what could possibly come out of it? Do I have the capacity to bear any more heartache? And so, I find myself writing here instead. Hoping it will lead to a catharsis of sorts.

VI. Swinging Backward
I thought I was getting better, but I recently discovered some notes/doodles he had secretly left me on my notepad the last time he spent the weekend with me. He seemed to know my love language so well! Sigh. How I wish he didn't, so this would be a lot easier.

VII. Swinging Forward
Of all the things I wish, one thought seems to emerge the most: I need to stop acting so bloody brave and really learn to protect my dear heart instead, i.e. maybe just listen to my friends next time.

LOVE DRUNK
I think I've fallen for you. I'm drunk on love and you're just drunk. I want you to change – change for me – because I know you could love me too. You know I'm good for you, I know you're bad for me, but I think together we could be something.

HARD TO GET

Unattainable love is hard to get over.

LOVE OF A LIFETIME

My phone rang: it was my love on my doorstep. Within minutes we were in each other's arms, and not long after that in bed together, skin to skin, energetically celebrating our reunion. It was four-and-a-half months since we had last touched one another's body, though over the last six weeks or so we had been finding that you can have a lot of bodily and emotional pleasure through communicating online. In this, and in other ways, our skills have improved with practice.

But there is nothing like the physical presence of the beloved, even when it is more than half a century since we first went to bed together. We both passed 70 a few years ago.

My love is in clerical orders. I am a pagan who has lately joined the Society of Friends. We live 400 miles apart, and my love has a spouse, so we don't get together that often, or as often as I would like. We love within limits, we have agreed. But we do love.

How long can this go on? My love's marriage has been on the line and they have been having relationship counselling: to end or mend? To leave a seven-year marriage is no light thing, especially when you are in holy orders.

In the meantime, we love and hold one another, and sing Tom Lehrer songs, and talk, and walk together in the sunshine when we can, eating ice cream.

Decisions are coming; but not yet.

But we do have a plan to meet next weekend!

MY PERFECT MATCH

So, I met this guy online, he seemed like my perfect match and made me feel amazing. We decided to meet, and I can safely say it has been the best three months ever. That was until I found out I was pregnant last week. Since telling him, he's done everything possible to guilt-trip me into having an abortion (even though I don't want one) and has become one of the most horrible people I've ever come across. Safe to say I'm heartbroken.

DOES IT MATTER?

We have been seeing each other for two years now. There was a time I couldn't imagine two weeks ahead. It's been a rollercoaster ride, a mad pendulum of 'Is this real? It can't be real. When will it end?'

You still won't hold my hand, and we have never said we love each other. But you tell me in other ways, I think. You care for me, and my friends, and my cat. Your family and friends know my name. We have stuck by each other. Even if it's circumstantial, we have chosen to continue, and we are silently committed to one another, I think.

Does it matter, then, that we only interlock fingers in the bedroom? That ours is a secret language? That I want to say I love you but I'm scared you'll run away? Does it matter that this might end eventually? Does this matter to you too?

IMPRINTS

My brain won't shut up from thinking about you. It's Christmas Day and, amongst all the chaos, I find myself wondering how your day is going; how you are doing; how things could have been. I still see you in all the syrup-swimming breakfast pancakes, the crackle-pop over-the-top fireworks, when Frodo stumbles into Mordor and when Harry finally defeats Voldemort. I wish I never learnt your kindness, your patience, your empathy. I wish I could go back in time and undo all the imprints you left on me.

ULTIMATES

We had been in and out of each other's lives for five years. Every time it ended it was always unresolved, and the time apart seemed to enable us even more but we had this intense, unbreakable connection. I snuck out last weekend to spend all night with him. We revealed things to each other that we thought were over but, obviously, are still alive and well.

Two days later, I told him that if there was no commitment, that would be it; no more contact. For the first time, we ended things amicably. We've grown and matured, but I've learnt that's not enough. I will always love him.

If I can't marry him, I'll travel and experience life to try to forget that the love of my life can't be with me.

LOCKDOWN BROUGHT ME BACK MY BEST FRIEND: UPDATE

A lot has happened. After New Year's Eve and deciding to see where this was going, we went back into lockdown. We continued to try to make things exciting while also getting to know each other better and agreed to do a date night every Saturday over Zoom. I got to know him for who he really was. In the past when we were friends, we hid so much from each other. I was so scared of my feelings, I never showed him the real me. It was like he was getting to know someone that was a stranger to him all those years ago. It was tough, especially with the added uncertainty of not knowing when we would be able to see each other again.

On Valentine's night, we got dressed up to sit in front of our computers and made a list of all the dates we wanted to go on when lockdown was over. We sent presents and cards to each other and agreed to open them together on Zoom. He sent me a framed picture that had the coordinates of where we first met in Turkey when we were eighteen years old. I was so overwhelmed, I burst into tears. It was the most thoughtful present anyone had ever given me. I realized I was completely in love with him. It hit me so hard, but I couldn't tell him over a video call, it wouldn't be right after all this time. I wrote him a letter to get it all out after the Zoom call so I knew how I felt in that moment and I could tell him when the time was right.

It got to early March and my birthday. We had gone nine weeks without seeing each other and decided to break the rules. I travelled to Bristol. We booked a hotel and planned a long weekend together. I was so nervous about seeing him. Only my closest friends and family knew I was going. I packed my bag, with my letter safely in there to give to him. I arrived in Bristol and there he was, waiting for me in real life. It was like a movie moment, we embraced and it felt like home.

It was my birthday the day I arrived, so we got to the hotel room and had some drinks. I opened my presents from him, and he then said, I need to talk to you about something. My heart froze, those dreaded words from someone. He said that he didn't want to mess around anymore and asked, would I commit to being his girlfriend? It was the quickest yes that I had ever said. I cried and said how happy I was. I felt that this was the moment to give him the letter I had written on Valentine's Day. I said to him, I don't expect anything back, but I want you to read this.

From this point, we have spent every other weekend travelling to see one another. It is hard at times and when we leave each other it really hurts, but I know this is all worthwhile because I have never felt like this in the past. We have spoken about how we are pleased it worked out this way because it allowed us to grow up and live our lives, which brought us back together at the right time.

There are no secrets anymore or hidden feelings, it's just natural and we click.

While in lockdown, we planned our first-ever date for when restrictions were lifted. We booked a restaurant in Bristol. It was the last week of May. I was so nervous but excited that we could sit in a restaurant together, not as friends, but finally as boyfriend and girlfriend. When I got to Bristol, he had taken a half day off work and booked a hotel. I arrived at the hotel room and he opened the door, and I saw that he had arranged rose petals on the floor, leading to a heart shape on the bed, where there was a bottle of my favourite wine and a letter. In the letter he said that he had never been able to be this open with anyone, he was so happy to know the real me after all these years, and he was even crazier about this version of me than the girl he knew at eighteen. He said he couldn't wait to build a future together, and in reply to my letter of March he said, I love you too.

Just over six months on, we are now planning a future together. Not only as best friends but partners, totally in love and me planning to move to Bristol from London by the end of the year.

Lockdown not only brought me back my best friend, but the love of my life.

MI AMOR

00:45 – Can I come over?
Fuck. Why do you do this to me? Why do I let you do this to me? Every single time I relapse.

02:15 – I'm here

Why can't my brain tell my body to stop finding you so attractive? Mierda.

I'm undressed within minutes and your body is pressed to mine, hands intertwined, your teeth sinking into my neck. Trembling as you caress every inch of skin, from my lips to my chest to my hips to my legs. Shaking as you tear into my back and leave little crescent bite marks across my shoulders. Donde quieres mis besitos?

Mi amor, why are you getting married to her next year?

AFTERGLOW

We slept together (again). Afterwards you said, 'it doesn't mean as much to me as it does to you'.

I need to stop letting you mess me up like this. Why am I such a fool?

MY PROBLEM

It's been three-and-a-half years. You said if it takes ten years, we'll be together. Am I doomed to wait until the decade mark, stuck in limbo? Rooted to this spot? My problem isn't that I won't love another. My problem is that I'll never love another as much. I'm afraid I'll never get over you. You. Haunt. Me.

DOES IT MATTER?: UPDATE

We had the chat. I didn't issue an ultimatum or anything. It wasn't dramatic. I just simply said what I wanted to you, one night, quietly. You acknowledged the fact that it had been unfair to me.

Today we hold hands as you walk me to the tube station before work. You've introduced me to your friends. We're going to meet my family over Christmas.

Don't get me wrong, it wasn't an overnight change just because of what I said. It's been months since that conversation and, slowly, things changed like the seasons do. And I think I love this season very much.

WANT TO BE

We are both hurting so much but I am paralysed with fear. You deserve to be with someone who will show you off to the world. My heart is broken, but I'm too afraid to be that person. I want to be. I want to be so badly.

HIM AND HER

We fell in love.

But you have her, and I have him.

FRIENDS & FAMILY

In a world of pop song love – where the dominant 'love' that we hear, see and culturally consume is the high of romantic love – the more constant (but by no means less deep, complex or meaningful) love of friends and family can feel like background noise; that it's always just *there*.

We have milestones in romantic relationships that are celebrated and become markers of lives: engagements, weddings, divorces – legal ceremonies and celebrations that seem to elevate the status of romantic love above other relationships. Yet, if we are lucky, friends grow up with us. They hold secrets and knowledge about us that can pre-date and outlast romantic relationships. Friends are the ones who often pick us up off the floor after a break-up, the ones we confide in, dissect dates, and sound out relationship troubles with. They support and stand by us. Even though the ending of friendships is not afforded the same cultural weight, discussion or space to grieve as the endings of romantic relationships, the loss of a close friendship can be just as painful.

When it comes to family dynamics, our relationships with parents are formative. We develop an attachment imprint with our primary carer in childhood and the repercussions of this, in our future relationships, are significant, often responsible for whether we approach romantic connections with anxiety, avoidance, security or disorganisation. Our relationships with our primary carers become our model of what love is, how it feels and operates, shaping our expectations of whether romantic connections are likely to be a source of security, suffocation, loss or instability. We often unconsciously replicate the dynamics we experienced in our childhood in our future romantic relationships. Understanding or unlearning relationship patterns from family members can be a complex process as their shadow is often cast deep into our lives. While romantic partners can come and go, our family is something we cannot choose.

And then there are the families that we make for ourselves, or want to: the pregnancies we long for, and the ones that surprise us. The grief of pregnancy loss and the inability to conceive. The internalised shame of infertility. The joy, jealousy and rage at witnessing friends' pregnancies when you are longing to conceive. The life shift of new parenthood: the rupture of identity, the sudden lack of freedom, the hysteria of sleep deprivation, the bodily drama, and slowly, the recalibration of a new self. These relationships change us to our core.

The stories in this chapter explore the love within friendships, family, and parenthood – the shifting in understanding between mothers and daughters over time, the complexities of grieving parents who didn't live up to their role in a traditional sense, the shame that can be carried down through generations, and the routes to healing. They articulate the anxiety, ambivalence, fierce desire, and lack of control in pregnancy, miscarriage, infertility and new motherhood. They celebrate friends over lovers – the friends who wait up until 3am just to give you a hug, the friends who never tire of playing Analyse Text; the friends whose wise words, quiet acts of unconditional support and chorus of laughter is the soundtrack to your best memories. The stories also articulate the lesser spoken about heartbreaks of friendships ending – the friendships that fade, the ghostings that cut deeper than the disappearances of lovers, the irrevocable loss of a best friend's sudden death, as well as the love they imbedded within you that transcends.

We are conditioned to seek, invest and focus on romantic love, but that doesn't mean we should save all our words for them. There are other people waiting to hear how we feel. Given the chance, before it's too late, what would you say?

THAT WAS LOVE

Somehow, I miss driving up the route 5, 115 degrees Fahrenheit outside, passing a rapidly melting frozen water bottle between the driver and passenger seats to hold against our temples and necks and cool us down. We could barely make out the voices of Bill Callahan and Palace Music over the hum of the engine of my shitty Volkswagen that would overheat after two minutes of running the air conditioning. It was too hot to talk but we'd scream over the wind rushing through the cracked windows when we needed to say something, or to say 'This one is so good' – 'What?' – 'THIS SONG IS GOOD'.

We didn't make many stops for fear of the car not starting again. We ordered horrible Chinese takeout from a sweet lady at a little pit-stop town off the freeway, who put our orange chicken and lo mein into a Styrofoam container. We sat in a parking lot, under the shade of an oak tree, cooling ourselves and the car down. You passed me a gloopy piece of broccoli and laughed as I turned it down, slumping over the pavement pretending to have heat stroke and singing 'Castaways' from the children's show *The Backyardigans*. I was exhausted and sad and desperate to be home but so happy to be there with you, making you laugh, loopy from heat and laughing too. That was love and I wish I had known it.

LITTLE BALL

At the beginning of the lockdown I had a miscarriage. I didn't know before my appointment. I went for the first routine scan and the doctor kept asking if my periods were regular, kept poking about and then just told me there was no heartbeat, the pregnancy wasn't going ahead and I also had a big cyst on my left ovary. Just like that. No sugar coating. I didn't really take it in initially, it was all so perfunctory. I saw the screen. I saw the still little ball that should have been my baby. The dark mass inside me. As I got dressed it sunk in and I silently sobbed behind the curtain as the doctor tapped away on the other side. She printed out the diagnosis letter and scan pictures. Told me I'd get a call when the operation to remove the miscarriage was booked. I took the papers and ran out the door, out the building, tears streaming down my face as I ran to my car where I sat and cried until I was able to see well enough again to drive home. The operation was the following week and until then I held it all together OK. The day of the op, I cried when I first got to the hospital and had to say what I was there for. A miscarriage. Even now, that word breaks my heart. When I woke up from the general anaesthetic and held my now-empty lower abdomen, I cried and cried. The nurses told me to get it all out. That evening, I felt like I'd been to a funeral – exhausted after a day of grieving.

Now I am fine most of the time, but not a day goes by when I don't think about my lost love, my baby, who I would have adored with all my heart: during quiet moments in early mornings before anyone else is up, when I'm in the shower, when I'm cooking. Sometimes I just collapse into a ball, unable to go on. I think about how I would have been so-many weeks pregnant by now and how big my belly should be. And now I just found out that the operation caused a big scar in my womb, which means I might not be able to get pregnant or carry a pregnancy to term again.

I have so much love for the baby I lost and for my unborn, yet-to-be conceived baby. Not knowing if I'll ever hold a newborn in my arms is breaking my heart every day. I dread the due date. I was counting on being pregnant again by then, but now that looks unlikely and I don't know how I'm going to get through it. My heartbreak is indescribable.

MOM

My mom was diagnosed with metastatic cancer in March. I went on a complete downward spiral of pain, fear, and anger because my relationship with her is not resolved. I destroyed my relationship with my boyfriend at the time, and since then have moved halfway across the world to be with my mom. Since being here, I've felt more alone than I care to admit – I have no friends around, can't speak the language and I'm stuck in confinement.

Everything looks fine on my social media. Some days I feel like an imposter... 'fake it until you make it', they say.

I am trying to become closer with my mom before it is too late, but I am also grieving never being able to have the mother I needed. It's a lot to feel at once, while caring for her day-to-day.

I am trying to rebuild myself and heal. It's really hard work. Some days are good, but most are a struggle. Showing up as my own mother, father, and nurturer and learning to love myself more every day.

TO EVERYTHING BUT YOU

I've written about ten drafts of this – in the hope that he'd read it and know I still loved him. After everything we went through, breaking up with him shattered everything inside me.

It's been six months and something has snapped. This love story is no longer about him. This is an ode to my amazing friends.

The friend that took me in with open arms and talked with me until 1 a.m., introduced me to a new side of London, watched me go mad on Japanese sake and made me smile again. The friend that helped me move into my new flat and did a healing spell for me, equipped with a sound bowl, pizza and wine. The friend that took me back to her home, after falling headfirst into the sandwich aisle in M&S, who still loves me and embraces my madness. The friend who made me my first roast of the year and danced with me round the living room. The friend who sends me near-daily funny memes and drinks wine with me down the phone.

And this love story is also dedicated to me: I'm growing into someone I like. I'm learning to cook for me, have therapy for me – not for him. I never thought I'd write a love story that wasn't about him. But to my friends: I love y'all.

BED SHARING

I spent the majority of my twenties sharing a bed with boys in some bid to find the personal calm that I now feel waking up to the face of my twelve-week-old baby. As promised, motherly love is like nothing else, and I was shocked at how hard it hit me. I've lost my identity and gained a new one in twelve weeks. Every morning I'm trying to work it all out while I look at his chubby little cheeks through sleep-deprived eyes.

Pregnancy and birth were a clusterfuck. Motherhood is equivalent to running a marathon, but instead of cheering you get everybody's opinion hurled at you from the sidelines. I've never been a runner.

Rushing through A&E on his fifth day, I had no idea what I was doing when they hooked the little man up to a tube, regularly taking his blood. 'I'm not cut out for this,' I repeated in my head over and over again. I sobbed on Day 7 as I pumped breast milk to go into the tubes. This was on a few hours' sleep after a traumatic birth.

But he made it through. After a four-night hospital stay, we were sent home. We have bonded and had the quiet time we both needed to get to know each other and heal. To learn how to be with each other. I'm fiercely territorial of him. I am reluctant to share him with anyone else. I'm not ready to come out of my bubble or to hear everyone else's opinions.

So I'll lie here and watch you sleep, little one, writing this story about how you taught me bravery, resilience and peace.

GIRL CODE

I first saw your comment on his Instagram photo and was drawn to the amount of kisses you left. You were flirty, which made me want to respond with 'Who are you and are you shagging him too?'. Instead, I opted for a not so subtle 'I thought we polished that wine off nicely last night'.

Instantly, my phone blew up. You never hurled abuse at me – all you wanted was answers. You listened and trusted me, before sharing your devastating side of the story. I heard all about the year-long relationship you had been having with him. We chatted long into the hours of Valentine's morning. We complimented each other, thanked each other for speaking and we not once blamed each other for his disgusting behaviour. I'm all about girl code and women lifting each other up, especially in their hour of need. This Valentine's was not quite what I expected. I fell more in love with girl code and strong women, and I hope she feels the same.

WHAT I KNOW ABOUT LOVE

When I had to move home, I decided to fly my cat (then just a kitten) with me since I couldn't bear the thought of leaving her in another continent for an unknown amount of time.

I've been back in my childhood home for four months now and I can't imagine how I'd cope if I didn't have her with me. My childhood was not particularly filled with love. My parents had an arranged marriage and it was made clear while I was growing up that we were not a family in which feelings were to be discussed.

This led to me having a profound hesitance of love, dating and serious relationships in my late teens and now early twenties. I don't know much about love, but I know that to have a healthy relationship you need to be able to be open about your feelings. This was something that I had no idea how to do. I felt a void and, because I knew I could never fill it with something steady and honest, I settled on sleeping with a string of random people.

This went on for a year or so until I realized that the void wasn't being filled and I still felt like shit. So, I decided to adopt a small black kitten. I honestly didn't think much of it when I brought her home, just that she'd give me some company when I was alone in an unfamiliar country.

The string of shitty hook-ups continued, but slowly I found myself feeling less shit about myself after the hook-ups left. My cat would jump up on my bed and rest her little head on my chest as if to say, 'It'll be alright, *you'll* be alright'.

Now that she's here with me she still does the same thing whenever I find myself upset over not being able to speak honestly to my family or if I'm having a down day.

I may still struggle with love and relationships, but one thing I know for sure is that I like myself more now, a year after adopting my furry companion, than I did before I brought her home on the bus.

THE WAIT

Schrodinger's Cat is a thought experiment: a cat is in a locked chamber, unobserved. According to the paradox, the cat is both alive and dead at the same time. Pregnancy is my Schrodinger's Cat. I've had several miscarriages but now I'm pregnant again. I can't see inside the locked chamber: the baby is there, and the baby is not there. I won't know for sure until a scan next week. Until then, I've been doing meditation, playing board games, drinking weak tea: trying not to press at the edges of the chamber. You are there and you are not. Love is acceptance of not knowing and of not having control.

FRIENDS OVER BOYS

My friend and I were talking the other day about how much we enjoy spending time with each other. I was planning on meeting her at the weekend before her

first date with this guy from Hinge – just to help her
get ready and have a few drinks to ease her nerves.
As we were chatting, she told me that she realized that
she doesn't really want to go and meet this boy and
would much rather spend time with me. I wanted to cry
because I felt so loved. And it made me realize that my
friendships will always be more important to me than
any boy.

Friends are people that you meet and enjoy their
company so much that you seek it out more. The phrase
'your friends are the family you choose' comes to mind
when I try to comprehend how spending quality time
with friends can lift my mood so much.

My friends are the true loves of my life.

DILDO DISCOVERY

In spring, my flatmate left for Switzerland. Dreamy, I
thought, the whole flat to myself! But that wasn't for
long: we agreed the room would be rented out as she
wasn't returning for a few months.

So, advert up. It felt weird choosing a stranger to live
with, but I found a great new girl from New Zealand who
seemed nice, easy-going and very relaxed. It seemed like
a good match.

Week one: maybe a bit too relaxed? At 11 p.m., she's
in the living room with the door shut. I could hear her
having a Zoom call. I needed to get a glass of water, which
meant walking through the living room. Well, I thought,
there's nothing wrong with knocking on the door and

walking in. 'Knock, knock, sorry to disturb!' I was surprised that she looked embarrassed... then I realized that she was sitting on the sofa dressed in sexy pyjamas, and there was a guy on her live chat.

Okay, I thought, she's a single lady, maybe she's lonely, maybe she's looking for adventure, she can video sex chat if she wants. I was very understanding. I quickly got my water and ran back to my bedroom (thinking: why is she doing this in the living room?).

The next day, 7 a.m. breakfast time: coffee mug in my hand, I slowly approach my comfy sofa and, before I sit down, I see it... clearly. A big, turquoise dildo fitted tightly inside the cavity of the sofa. OMG... I thought! She's not just left it there but also totally forgotten about it?! I just hoped that she would see it later, remove it and never do it there again.

I come back from work... dildo still there.

I hadn't anticipated having to ask my new flatmate to kindly remove a sex toy from the living room. After a hundred rehearsed conversations in my head, I decided just to pray to God that she would finally see it and move it.

A day later: she's moved cushions to cover it up!

Dildo day 3: I've had enough! I'm going to removed it myself! I hope it is not stuck there permanently! I'll put it on her bed, she has to learn, and she can be embarrassed forever. Shame on you, I thought. With bare hands, I approached the green monster, like King Arthur pulling out Excalibur. Instead I pulled out... my dog's rubber TOY.

Yes indeed...

The happiness my dog felt at being reunited with her lost dog was insane! I was crying tears of joy that I hadn't sent my flatmate an embarrassing message or had a serious conversation with her about it. On the other hand, maybe she'd thought the same thing about me! That it was my toy and she was covering it up – thinking, when will I finally notice it?

We're still friends.

NOT ANOTHER BREAK-UP SONG

There is a lot that we have agreed on recently: the *Gavin and Stacey* Christmas Special was an absolute success, Little Mix are the best girl band ever, Taylor Swift is misunderstood and unfairly villainized, we both seriously miss McDonald's nugs, and we should never have fallen out.

This isn't just any love story, it's a friendship love story.

We were the girls who shouldn't have been friends (in fact, we were pretty indifferent to each other when we first met). Me blonde, tanned and in crop tops come rain or shine; you super-cool Mod with the beehive to go with it and practically allergic to the sun. I LOVE commercial music; you are an indie kid through and through. I am super-blunt and upfront; you will avoid confrontation at any cost. I love a night in Soho (coming home at 6 a.m. on a Sunday morning when we lived together was a standard); you liked a nice cosy drink in a cute pub.

And what brought us back together? The *Gavin and Stacey* Christmas Special. Of course, we both loved it and absolutely had to speak about it. We are brain twins. So many times we will be going to text each other about the same thing, will be listening to the same song at the same time. Remember that coaster I bought you that you had seen the day before and wanted but didn't buy and the next day, without you mentioning it, I had bought it for you as I thought you'd like it?

I promise I will always pour a drink over a guy who is rude to you (true story) and I know you will always tolerate how mainstream I am.

To quote Charlotte in *Sex and the City*, 'Maybe we could be each other's soulmates. And then we could let men be just these great, nice guys to have fun with.' And let's be fair, A. and C. will have to be OK with that because they know what they signed up for when they met us.

This is probably the most romantic thing I have ever done. Bring on Galantine's!

ALL THE SINGLE LADIES

I recently got my hair cut. It's been two years and I had outgrown the long blonde ponytail with its frizzy ends. Without a doubt, getting one's hair cut after a break-up has become a tale as old as time. I had broken up with my boyfriend, but this did not affect me much. Call me cold-hearted, but there are break-ups more severe than this.

It's been a day since I left my old flat. I'd been living there with my best friend for over a year, sitting outside on the balcony in a daze of smoke and booze, proclaiming whole-heartedly, like clockwork, every night 'Those are the nights!', screaming wildly at each other when playing cards, and calling her out for waving around her pizza crust when giving me advice, reading stories to one another, and being shushed by the neighbours.

Now I've packed up my life in three suitcases and will move to London in a couple of weeks.

I've been reading Traister's *All the Single Ladies: Unmarried Women and the Rise of an Independent Nation* and there's a chapter on female friendships, which, taken from a letter by Charlotte Brontë, are like Lucifer's Matches. They're dangerous and unsettling to the traditional, patriarchal view of the nuclear family and heteronormative expectations of marriage and childbirth. I want neither of these things. Essentially, the idea is that female friendships are sometimes more formative than actual relationships, because they offer different systems of support, of sharing experiences, of stimulation.

'Female friendship was not some consolation prize, some romance also-ran. Women who find affinity with each other are not settling. In fact, they may be doing the opposite, finding something vital that was lacking in their romantic entanglements, and thus setting their standards healthily higher.' (Rebecca Traister)

In this light, love's labour's lost on me; the perils of flicking through humourless and idiotic Tinder bios, or Tinder bios that try so hard not to be humourless and idiotic; or staying in an unsatisfying relationship out of comfort. All of this is lost on me. Don't get me wrong; I miss the thrills of going out, I miss flirting, and I miss sex. But I know that all this will come back, in a new city, in some months, whenever, wherever.

In relationships, I look for temporary companions, with whom I can share a span of my life, but for whom I'd never sacrifice even the slightest portion of my freedom. Since I do not want to marry, or bear children, or fulfil any conventional life path that seems set in stone, this is exactly my deal. But friendships, such connections, such love, such chosen kin, transcend every boundary, even the big sea between a small German town and the Big Smoke. We might continue our studies in different countries, start our career in different cities, publish books at different times, will scream at other people when playing cards, we might settle in relationships, or start families and defy all of our rebellious stances from now, but none of that matters, because our dearest people, whoever they may be, are only a video call away, whenever, wherever. And from now on, I'll be sharing my bottle of red with my gal from across a screen, because I know this will last a lifetime. To female friendships, cheers!

CLINK TOGETHER

My mom and I have made it a practice to go for walks together. So, yesterday, right on schedule, we went for our daily walk. She talked as I nodded and added an occasional comment or story in between her streams of consciousness. That's usually how our conversations go. We've gotten into the groove of it.

But yesterday was different. As my mom was on her third stream of consciousness she choked up, which she rarely does anymore. She opened up to me about how she doesn't feel heard in her marriage. There's a lack from my father... 'a dismissiveness', she explains. I know exactly what she's talking about the second she says it.

'He always pegs me as annoying or waves me off,' she chokes back even more tears.

Then, out of what felt like a wave of the purest form of love, she stops walking and whispers, 'I am so lucky to have such an amazing daughter.'

I nod and wrap my arm around her. We're both skinny. Our bony arms clink together, making it impossible for me to convey just how tightly I want to hold her in that moment.

'When you were younger you didn't hear me either... I tried, but you dismissed me too. It hurt.'

I go to reply, but she interrupts me:

'That's besides the point.'

We walk with a new understanding hanging over us.

THIS IS NOT YOUR TYPICAL LOVE STORY

It's my granny's birthday today. She is my best friend. Was my best friend.

It's coming up to a year since she passed away and I'm struggling. She was my biggest love, and the lady who always made the best Sunday lunch and the most fantastic memories.

Her laugh would always fill a room, no matter how big or small; her presence was undeniable. She was the typical granny in the sense that I would never leave her house unfed, and she would always pass me some money with a 'don't tell anybody else about this' kind of arrangement. I was the tall to her small – the top shelves were my area and the bottom shelves hers.

I miss the standard routine we had. I'd ask if she had any biscuits (which she always had – packets and packets unopened) and she'd reply saying that there might be some. I'd top up the biscuit tin and bring it in to her with a cup of coffee (cream instead of milk if she was feeling extra fancy that day – and always one sugar). We'd share our stories (she once got stuck driving in a blizzard on the way to the cinema with her friends) and we'd watch *Escape to the Country* and imagine it was our life.

There's so much love I have left for her, and so much more I want to give. But I can't. She's not here in body and I can't hug and cry with her spirit.

I'm trying to be half the woman she once was – I just hope that's enough.

GIRL GANG

This last year brought me a new girl gang with the most beautiful, kind-hearted souls I've ever met. Sometimes I think we forget that some of the best kind of love is the love received by our friends.

THIS IS A LOVE STORY

This isn't your average love story, but it's a love story nonetheless. It's a story about friendship.

We met on SpareRoom in February and within a week I'd moved in. You had only moved in a month before, but when I came to view the flat, something clicked into place. Fast forward five months and we know each other inside and out. Five months of talking, laughing, crying, hugging, napping, gardening, cooking, drinking, dancing, endless games of cards and all the wine.

You've helped me through my struggles more than you'll ever know. Friendship is everything, and we found exactly that.

You're a gem, one of the rarest kinds. I'll forever be grateful that I was one of the lucky ones that found you.

CLOSER

We're close friends. You used to confide in me about everything... but you have a new person to confide in, another closer friend. I'm jealous. I wish I wasn't. I just remember how that used to be me.

BEYOND

To the love that can spend six hours on the phone, having spent the whole day together. To the love of the *Back to the Future* series (that will always take me back to lying in front of the TV in your living room back home). To the love that can bridge countries and continents. To a love that can get over kissing the same teenage heartthrob (sorry). To the love that knows no bounds, and no judgement. To years of unconditional support, whenever and wherever you need. To a love that will last as long as we can imagine. To my best friend – to fifteen more years and beyond.

THE DARK SIDE

This is a story about love. But not the romantic kind. The kind you have with friends. The kind that uplifts you in all ways. But what happens when that love isn't there for you in the darkest of times? When you need that love the most and instead you feel lonelier than ever. Sometimes, love changes or better said, people change. Sometimes, the dark, horrible, bitter side was always there.

Friends are supposed to be your biggest supporters. Your biggest fans. Your go-to. If you can't have that in your toughest moments, when can you? I realized the darkness in our friendship had always been there, yet it took me being at my lowest to see it. That the love was only one-sided.

This is a story of a break-up. A break-up of friendship. Don't let anyone dim your light.

COFFEE CAKE

I want to start by saying I'm not a coffee drinker.
I don't like it: as a drink, in chocolates, even in a
cocktail. When you made that amazing-looking cake
and asked me if I wanted a slice I, of course, said yes.
Just as I was about to take a bite I asked the flavour,
you said coffee... I prepared myself to fake a smile
and pretend it was delicious. I took a bite... and it
was the best thing I've ever tasted. Perfection. And
that was the thing about you, you made everything
wonderful.

We were kindred spirits. You were my sister's best
friend; but someone I could easily count as a friend of
my own. We had a nickname where we combined our
names because we had the same thoughts on everything
– such was the fact that if one of us had an opinion on
something, the other would think the same. It was an
ongoing joke in our WhatsApp group and when we'd all
hang out at parties. We laughed at the same things, rolled
our eyes at the same people, and definitely did NOT
approve of that married guest at the wedding flirting
with every woman he could find.

You were so cool – not in an intimidating way, but
effortlessly so. You had no idea how badass you were.
You did things your way. You joked that you blended into
the crowd, but everyone you met loved you; the girl with
the amazing curly hair, the perfect smile and the kindest,
purest heart.

You were a couple of weeks away from realising your
dreams and that's why it's so cruel that you're gone.

It hasn't hit me properly yet, I just can't compute it – who will I sit next to at the next social gathering to guarantee I have a great night? Who will come out with the same sarcastic, no BS advice as me? Who will be there as the friend that everyone needs?

I'll probably never have coffee cake like yours again. Like you, it was one of a kind.

HERE

I miss my best friend. It's been a long time but I'm still here, ready whenever you are.

GREATEST LOVES

Me and my two best friends might not have been able to see each other this year, but we have spoken every day without fail (thank the technology gods for WhatsApp). We have known each other thirteen years, and been through everything together. This last year we have all experienced some challenging and life-changing times.

One of them moved country to be with her boyfriend. The other got married and had baby number three. I got the job of my dreams.

Even with those big, life-changing events, we have been with each other every step of the way through the big and small, and I couldn't be more grateful. We've supported each other through emotional breakdowns (home-schooling incidents, being stuck in a country without the love of your life, near panic attacks, mass diarrhoea episodes, taxis across the country to get away from boyfriends, and the worst hangovers ever – yep they've been broad) and we are stronger than ever.

I love them so very, very much. And they will be my greatest love story of all time, forever.

THE ONLY ONE

Being a single parent to a baby that turned into a toddler... watching her grow, learn, laugh and somehow falling even more wholly, deeply and completely in love with her all over again.

It's been hard. But it's been beautiful.

That's my love story. And it's the only one I want.

GHOSTS AND SOULMATES

I don't believe in soulmates in the same way I don't believe in ghosts. I loudly proclaim their nonexistence because I choose to live my life avoiding the notion that I might run into one. Those unrealistic expectations and unnecessary paranoid thoughts are not welcome here, no thank you. That being said, if one (soulmate, ghost, or ghost soulmate alike) happens to emerge from the mysteriously sealed door in my bedroom I will gladly reconsider my beliefs. Until then I will spend my days accompanied by boxed wine and my roommates; the best roommates I could have asked for, including my best friend of twenty-one years.

Her and I have survived kissing the same boy, appearing unbearably weird to our peers, and living together during a global pandemic. Our friendship is one of the things I am most proud of and I find myself talking about her the way a retired war veteran would talk about his wife of fifty-plus years. We may have not persevered through war, but have lasted through the tortuous years of high school and an unforgiving puberty of braces and awkwardness. I wish there were a small story that perfectly encompassed our friendship, but our memories are endless scatterings across my life.

My tall, free-spirited, loving friend and I share so many of the same memories that she almost feels like an extension of myself. She taught me how to speak bravely and thrift passionately and cook creatively. She taught me how to write down my goals for grade 10 then burn them so they felt less scary. That winter day her mom came home to us running and shrieking outside in our swimsuits as we felt reborn as liberated women. She will always hug me hello and goodbye. She will always listen to my woes. She will always make me feel accepted for the person I am. We are at our best dancing in sweaty clubs and using our 'boxing out' basketball skills to fend off unwanted male attention. We are at our best sitting over a delightful pastry and chatting at an inappropriate volume. Heck, we are at our best wearing bright surgical gloves to match our face masks and navigating our way around the grocery store aisles. It seems even a global pandemic can be fun as long as we are together and fill our days dancing to empowering music, rewatching rom-com classics from the early 2000s, and dreaming of our futures.

It often feels reminiscent of our small-town summers, when we had little to no stressors and endless time to share. Most days were spent sitting side by side on a dock, looking out at the lake, and thinking of all the directions our lives could go. Just two girls feeling entirely at the mercy of the waves and the world but thankful for yet another successful trip to the beach. We may have graduated from uncool, scared-of-boys high schoolers, but we are still the same two weird dreamers, just slightly older and slightly wiser as we look out at our unknown futures from inside our shared basement suite.

Right now, my tomorrows feel uncertain but I cannot complain about my todays. We can be found laughing louder than our landlord would like, arguing over if Chad Michael Murry is good-looking, and signing yet another year's lease. Once again, we have all the time in the world. I might even revisit my idea of what a soulmate is, do a quick Google search for a suitable definition, and check that sealed door in my bedroom in case ghosts do in fact exist.

ANTS

It's so funny how I have written multiple stories about the boy I loved for six months and not one about the girl I loved for six years. Until now.

When the word 'ex' is brought up, the majority of afflictions are levied on failed romances: the partner that couldn't commit or the lover that cannot compromise. But what about the ex-best friend?

The break-up with, or rather ghosting, of the ex-best friend cuts deep, when you least expect it; the trinkets scratch at the surface, reminding, reminiscing, romanticising.

This isn't a conventional 'love' story. It's a story about picking out ants from the pineapples we bought off a side-stall in Asia; it's trying to calm the taxi-woman down while you're in the back seat of her car trying not to throw up; it's the dirty old men who brought over an extortionate-priced amount of champagne for us to devour; it's the lying on the dewy grass outside the funfair with the sun seeping into our skin; it's the taste of that awful mixture of sambuca and Rennie; it's the swaying of our hips in our denim shorts at the summer music festival with cigarette smoke in our lungs; it's the learning life through living with you.

How petty it seems to be loving a six-month boy who never loved me back, when a six-year love ended just like that.

ONE TRUE LOVE

I've moved on from dreaming about my exes to dreaming about my mum. I guess if you give it long enough, with enough distance, the one true love story of your life will always come through.

THE LAST ONE

The last one of my child-free friends has given birth.

My partner and I have been trying for three years now. At our 13th March 2020 appointment, we chose to postpone our IVF referral by two months to wait for our perfect clinic that offered funding. We thought it was a good idea, until lockdown meant the clinics closed and appointments were delayed. Tests 'expired' and needed redoing. Waiting lists grew and grew. I silently struggled watching my friends with newborns and growing bumps joining The Mum Club.

Then suddenly things were moving again. Scans, injections, tablets, injections, scans, injections. Egg retrieval. And after all of that, one single, little embryo.

Next month we transfer our one and only embryo and pray it sticks around.

EVERYTHING (LITTLE BALL: UPDATE)

An update. I wrote here about the miscarriage I had. I'm now sitting up awake in the middle of the night nursing my newborn. My love is overflowing and endless. She's not just a baby. She's everything.

I CAN STILL REMEMBER

I can remember the exact moment I first saw her.

It was my first week of university. I walked into the shared kitchen of our halls of residence, and she was standing at the back of the room, drying a saucepan with a dish towel, her dark hair tied up in a high ponytail. That's her; that's my best friend, I thought. We'd never spoken, I didn't know anything about her and yet in that moment I knew this fact as clear as if it was my own name. I guess this is what some people call love at first sight.

I am bad at selecting suitable men to date, but famously brilliant at choosing friends. I wasn't wrong that day in the kitchen, she really did turn out to be the best friend I'd ever have.

We lived together in halls, we lived together in a student house, we lived together after we graduated in our first rented flat.

Once upon a time, at university, I texted her on a night out to say that I had seen the boy I was sort of seeing kissing his ex in the union. She waited up in our kitchen until I got home at 3 a.m. just to give me a hug before she went to bed. That was the kind of friend she was. That was the best hug of my life.

In many ways we were different, but we fit together because we both valued and invested in friendship as much as romantic love. In fact, more so.

I adored her and was fascinated by her because she thought differently to other people. She was so knowing, with such a quiet strength. She was so wise, so content and so unashamedly herself. Sometimes I'd interview her, record our conversations and transcribe them as works of art because she blew my mind.

She was the most present friend, there no matter what. She'd turn up to my art performances alone, just to be there for me. She never got bored of playing Analyse Text. She gave the best advice. Was on my side. She was my best friend. My bridesmaid. A godparent to my first child. But so much more. She was my safe space and I was hers. For eighteen years I had her back and she had mine.

I never took her for granted, but I took for granted that she would always be in my life. That part I got wrong. Five days before we were last due to meet up for coffee, twelve days into her feeling on and off ill with flu-like symptoms, she was found dead at home. She was thirty-five years old, with no underlying health conditions, and she died.

She was in the process of adopting a baby as a single woman because that's how badass and determined she was. She believed that you need no one but yourself to fulfil your dreams, and so that was how she lived. She was just three weeks away from finally meeting her little girl, which makes the universe taking her even more cruel.

I'm so glad that she knew how much I loved her because, much to her amusement, I told her all the time. Apparently, grief is the price we pay for love, which is why my heart is broken.

It's been three years now. I hate that it keeps getting longer. It still doesn't feel normal – thankfully. I don't want it to ever feel normal.

'How do you get over something?' I once asked her.

'You don't,' she said. 'I don't think that's the point. You just take it into you and you adapt and it becomes a part of who you are.'

Every now and then, I dream about her. Last night I dreamt of her again. In the dream she was somehow both alive and dead. We hugged and hugged and hugged. I never wanted to let her go.

IN A RELATIONSHIP

Social media is awash with relationship posts: from soft-launching new ones to engagement announcements and wedding-day pictures. But we aren't as exposed to the disintegration of relationships, nor the everyday banalities that may not be aesthetic but can be the cement of long-term love.

Likewise, film and popular culture often focus on the quest to getting into a relationship, but not what happens once you're in one. The everyday, undramatic workings of relationships often go unrepresented, and yet this is how the majority of our time in a relationship is spent.

Being in a relationship can be a source of support and security. It can be strengthening and elevating. But that's not the only story. It can also be a source of anxiety and ambivalence, and without public exposure to those realities, experiencing that can feel isolating.

Even the best relationships are triggering. They hold up a mirror to our unconscious beliefs, strengths and insecurities, and bring carried wounds that we have not yet healed to the surface, and then they face those of our partner's. When two people's needs, desires and skillsets complement one another, the coupledom you have co-created can be both soothing and expansive, but when they clash it can start to feel more like a battle. One that may or may not be worth having.

We never fully know what another couples' relationship is like. By their nature, relationships are exclusive experiences lived by the people within the couple. Romantic relationships are a strange mixture of public and private, and this friction can lead to us viewing others' relationships through a strangely competitive lens, where we can project, judge and fantasise from the outside, and hold our lived, known and complex experience of being in a relationship against us. In the age of social media, this is amplified and can lead to us both performing our relationships for external viewers, and only consuming the glossy parts of others' relationships: a toxic combination for enabling false comparisons. Because of this, revealing the true nature of your relationship to others can feel exposing, causing us to only share certain aspects, which further perpetuates the skewed views and expectations we have of romantic relationships. It can be hard to hold on to the fact we are only ever seeing fragments of other people's relationships, which should be no barometer for ours, yet we viscerally experience the multifacets of our own.

The stories in this chapter explore the nuances of being attached: the shifts in long-term love and how it feels to fall out, as well as into, love. They celebrate the mundane acts that glue people together, as well as revealing the shadow sides of relationships that we often repress – confusion, ambivalence, pretence. They speak of the internal conflict of trying to work out when a relationship is over or if it's still worth the fight. They articulate the shock, grief and recalibration of the self and the partnership when faced with revelations that come seemingly out of the blue. They speak of private fears and conflicting desires, but also of synergies and celebrations. These are stories of falling apart, and of working together.

ONCE UPON A TIME

There was once a time you excited me, when you stirred up a storm in my bones. But now the waters are still and my body keeps pulling away from you.

Is this what it feels like to fall out of love?

SOMETIMES I LIE

I must admit that sometimes I lie in bed with my boyfriend and think about my ex. How he never quite gave me what I wanted and never really showed me the respect I deserved, yet I was always chasing him.

To this day I still chase him, under the guise of friendship. I never tell my boyfriend we are meeting. My ex and I gossip and giggle for a few hours and discuss each other's love lives. I always feel like there is a competitive tone, but I might be reading into it. Sometimes I watch his beautiful lips spew out the most egocentric crap I've ever heard, yet for some reason I fall in love with him all over again.

After four or five hours of his company, we run out of things to say and get bored. We part ways and agree to meet again in a few months' time. I'm always left feeling deflated, brought back to reality, realising that love is so much more than the longing for what you can't have. It's about stability, security and real genuine friendship.

My boyfriend is in the dark about our meetings and I think I'll keep it that way. Why ruin something amazing for the sake of reigniting an old flame, which clearly never burned so brightly in the first place?

Being in love is complex and if I'm honest, I'm in love with them both.

RUNNING

I became a different person when the trauma I'd been running from caught up with me. Eight years of working solidly, socialising and exercising suddenly stopped, and I wasn't the girl you fell in love with any more. I was no longer gregarious and outgoing and confident. I was stuck in the dark, with a duvet over my head, unable to face the day. I was running compulsively until I tore the muscle in my calf. I could feel his hands on me, not yours.

Then I started therapy. Things got worse before they got better, but you loved every version of me. You were there every step of the way as I found myself again. I had a whole new outlook on us, and what we could do together. Then we found out we were going to be parents. It was a hard pregnancy and a difficult birth, but you've loved this new version of me just as much.

I KNOW

I've spent almost half of my life with him. We're inexplicably intertwined. I love him, I do.

But I know he's not the love of my life.

I TELL HIM I ENJOY EVERY MINUTE

I moved in with my relatively new boyfriend and I tell him I enjoy every minute of it. In reality, I'm riddled with anxiety. I feel trapped in a cage and far from home. He so adamantly loves me and thinks we are going to spend the rest of our lives together. As much as I adore him, I fear we are too young to make such commitments to each other.

I went through his ex-girlfriend's messages with him and it's all the same: 'can't wait to get our dream house and a puppy.' Sometimes I worry if he's being genuine with me or just acting out what he thinks love is from interpretations from popular culture. I hate the fact that what I thought were our dreams have come from a script he's used before.

If anyone asks, moving in together has really helped me get to know him and it's beautiful. In reality, I've realized no matter how unhappy my gut feeling is, I'll always be a co-dependent motherfucker.

SYMBIOTIC

With him being made redundant and me being busier than ever, our dynamic has changed.

He gets out of bed early so that he can wake me up with a cup of tea. He goes for walks and comes home with books I might enjoy. He brings me cold glasses of water when I'm happily sweating in the bathtub. He takes time cooking dinner, carefully considering what I might like, and then does the washing-up, too. He makes me hot-water bottles when I've been working so long in the same position that I've become an icicle. He drags me away from my computer at lunchtime to make me go for a walk, then holds my hand inside his coat pocket. He makes me Marmite toast even though he hates the smell.

He looks after me, even though he's struggling too.

SCARED

We have been together for five years, and he's grown into someone I can't love.

He told me he's scared to be alone. I'm so scared.

NIGHT

My heart aches at night as I lie next to you, hoping you'll hold me.

PUT A RING ON IT

Reaching four years together, I was expecting wedding commitments. I expressed this to him and said that I felt it important to get to the next step, otherwise I would need to move on. He agreed and told me soon after Christmas that he had bought a ring. Three months later and still no proposal; apparently the ring was stuck at the border due to 'customs problems'.

One night: a big argument. He left me and cut his phone off for a week without any explanation. He came back and told me there never was any ring, he just didn't want to break up and didn't want to hurt me. He tells me that he's going to Mexico for two weeks and we should see where we are when he comes back.

It's been four months and he's not come back yet.

But since he's been gone, I've met someone who is committed to me, who is not scared to express his feelings, who loves me and tells me that he wants to build a future with me and get a dog. So, you can stay in Mexico.

DYNAMIC

He taught me to change my car tyres so I can be strong and independent. But he also says I don't have to, because he wants to do things for me. He's patient and kind. He's everything I didn't know existed and didn't believe I deserved. It's been six months of trust and friendship and good communication. And now we're looking to buy a place together.

MODERN FAIRY TALE

I'd lost all hope. I thought true love didn't exist. I told my gran at Christmas that I'll have to just settle for another idiot and would probably never have kids.

We met in December and couldn't be apart, so moved in together before we'd even had sex. But when we did it was incredible. We knew we were meant to be together. With me being older and unsure of my fertility, we decided to try for a baby. Little did we know, our little girl was already there with us.

I will always tell my daughter, what you want *does* exist – and the longer you waste with the wrong person is less time available to find your soulmate. If there's even a doubt in your mind, he's not The One. Move on. He's out there, don't worry.

LOVE ADDICT

I met a guy and fell head over heels in love. In a whirlwind, we decided to move in together. A few days into living together, I found out he was a heroin addict.

I don't know why I didn't walk away at that point, but something kept me there. My life became chaos, and our relationship was a mess, but I honestly believed that the pain of trying to help him would hurt less than the pain of heartbreak. It took him going to rehab, relapsing straight on release and him moving into a homeless shelter for me to finally realize how bad things were. And now I'm on the other side, I can't believe what he put me through, what I put myself through. He's gone now and I'm healing every day.

YOU'RE SO COOL

Me and my boyfriend have been together for five years. We were both off work for a month at the same time and had the best time. We went for walks, hung out in the garden and binge-watched TV box sets. It was so fun, like a trial run for retirement. We're best friends and even now I look at him and think, 'You're so cool.'

SOUR-DOUGH

Who would have thought it
But we've baked sourdough loaves
More than we've made love.

40 YEARS

We spent our time hiking, watching Netflix films and nature documentaries. He read, I sewed, we talked, cooked, and frequently tried out new recipes. I thought our marriage was OK.

Then two days before Valentine's Day, we went for a walk and he told me our marriage had run out of road, that we did not have enough shared interests and that he did not want to spend his remaining years of good health with me. We would have been married for forty years next month.

He refused to go to couples counselling. The day after Valentine's Day he instructed a solicitor. Family life has been blown apart, our children are estranged from him, and he has not seen our grandchildren in weeks.

I have never cried so much in my life. But I am so fortunate to be supported by our children, my extended family, and absolutely wonderful friends. I've discovered I am stronger than I ever thought I could be. And I've been feeling my way towards a different future.

Now comes the plot twist. He has just told me he loves me truly and deeply, he has made a massive mistake and that it has all been like a dream he's just woken up from. What do I do now?

STEREOTYPES

There are stereotypes about two women in love: intense emotions, fast-paced relationships, and the acquiring of walking boots and cats. We've successfully achieved them all in our four years together.

If fulfilling those stereotypes is meant to be a bad thing, then really, I feel sorry for straight people. I've never loved long walks, our cat, or just being with her – chatting for hours on end – more.

THE RIGHT THING

I have been in a long-distance relationship with my boyfriend for over a year now; for the majority of our relationship. After five months, I finally flew out to see him and had the most perfect two weeks... until I saw that he had been texting another girl for nudes – both receiving and sending them. I immediately flew home as I was so heartbroken, but after two weeks of being apart I'm flying out to see him again. He's trying to fix his mistakes as I know he's truly sorry for what he's done. Am I right to give him a second chance?

SWEPT AWAY

I never imagined that two years after meeting you we'd be welcoming a beautiful baby girl into our lives. We have been each other's rock since the day we met. We've supported each other through redundancies, job changes, self-doubt, and periods of poor mental health.

We have debated things, had disagreements, moments of not talking – but all that gets forgotten. It is swept away with the endless amounts of laughter, happy tears, the many 'firsts' and making memories that will last forever.

Now, more than ever, you are my rock. We share a baby girl who is nearly five months old and throughout my postnatal depression, you stand strong next to me. I have in you a soulmate for life. A bond that will last forever. I'd never have thought a dating app would lead me to you.

THANKS

Thank you for smiling your charming smile that night when our electric feelings vibed.

Thank you for smiling the same smile again the next time too.

Thank you for walking me home to make sure I was safe.

Thank you for messaging me after, striking up great conversation and keeping me hooked.

Thank you for messaging me again, even after I went silent.

Thank you for chasing me until I was ready to love.

Thank you for the endless compliments.

Thank you for exciting day trips and surprise bookings abroad.

Thank you for loving me.

Thank you for moving in with me, making my house feel like a home.

Thank you for introducing me to a whole host of new experiences.

Thank you for the nights cooking delicious food together.

Thank you for engulfing me in your family. They truly are the best.

Thank you for making me the proudest auntie of your beautiful niece and nephew. God, how I love them.

Thank you for planning our future together – forever and always.

Thank you for making me feel so bloody lucky.

Thank you for being my jigsaw piece, fitting my heart so perfectly.

Until you didn't fit any longer.

Thank you for the late nights when you didn't come home.

Thank you for the worry.

Thank you for making me wonder why I wasn't good enough.

Thank you for the confusion.

Thank you for getting outrageously drunk far too often. So drunk that you couldn't control your own bodily functions or temper.

Thank you for always blaming me.

Thank you for twisting truths and telling your friends.

Thank you for the no apologies.

Thank you for calling me disgusting names.

Thank you for the silent treatment.

Thank you for being 'too tired' to be close.

Thank you for ruining our trips away.

Thank you for embarrassing me in front of others.

Thank you for regularly cancelling plans.

Thank you for ignoring the tears I tried to stifle as I lay next to you at night.

Thank you for kicking me out of your car and telling me to get the bus home.

Thank you for being a complete arse to my closest friends.

Thank you for moving the goalposts on our future plans.

Thank you for never committing.

Thank you for breaking your promises.

Thank you for making me feel like I was asking for too much after 'only four years'.

Thank you for being bitter about paying me rent.

Thank you for making me feel like the loneliest person in the world.

Thank you for realising what you had once it was too late.

Thank you for destroying my heart, over and over again.

Thank you for showing me both what love can be and what love should not be.

Thank you for everything.

I thank myself for seeing things clearly and understanding that an amazing beginning doesn't excuse a miserable present.

I thank myself for finding the strength to ask you to leave, despite loving you with my whole heart.

I thank myself for remaining strong when you tried to come back again and again.

I thank myself for wishing you the best.

I thank myself for no longer loving you.

I thank myself for allowing myself the time and space to grieve my once niece and nephew. I miss those little beauties so much. My little lost loves; my hardest heartbreak. I'm over you but I'm not over them.

DIFFERENT PLACES

We're in two different places, physically and mentally, and while this makes me scared to lose him, I'm not sure he feels the same way.

HANDS

I was mesmerised by your beautiful hands when I first met you: the elegant way you gesticulated and used them to express yourself.

Now, twenty-five years later, those hands have cupped my face, pulled me close, slipped a ring on my finger, cradled our children, made our house a home. I still enjoy drifting off to sleep with a hand encased in yours.

THE ONE WITH THE HAPPY ENDING

I have spent a lot of the time being haunted by the ghosts of past boyfriends, replaying relationships in my head like old episodes of *Friends*:

- The one with the manipulative control freak
- The one with the aggressive drunk
- The one where I waited for eight years
- The one that could have been but never was

Time has also given me the chance to process feelings I didn't know I was harbouring, but let's face it, no one wants to watch these episodes – these are the ones you skip through to get to the Thanksgiving special.

I now feel like I can finally leave the past where it belongs. Which is lucky, as it turns out while I had spent my spare time dissecting my past, my boyfriend had been busy planning our future, and writing his own episode – the one with the proposal.

THE HYPE

I moved in with a boyfriend that I had met only five weeks earlier. Being older, we thought 'This is it'. It soon became apparent he had a drinking problem. Weeks later, it turned out to be a drug addiction too, with a good mix of emotional abuse.

While I was being a good step-mum and housewife, posting pictures of dogs and baking with his kids, really, I was miserable, traumatised and just trying to keep his kids happy and fed. I am happy to say that I left him in June and life since, on my own in my safe happy home, is better than settling for any scraps of love from someone else. Don't believe the hype.

RAFTS

We fell out of 'just friends' and into love three years ago, having met at work and enjoying each other's kind and silly company. We moved into our first house at the end of last year, then by March we were locked down into it. We'd gone from opposite shifts to 24/7 contact and it was bliss. A holiday together in our own new home – what could be better?

But, as the weeks turned into months, the worry of redundancy, competition for jobs, friends and family slipping out of existence to this new illness, and the chaos of the outside world left us clinging to each other on an isolation raft.

He sank into a sadness unlike anything I'd known him to experience before. He's a light-up-the-room kind of guy, and this was a change that tested us both by pushing at our innermost weaknesses. It was such an intense closeness to another person's struggles that the fear of discovering darkness in the person you love, and in yourself, began to creep in.

After a few weeks of silence and tears, sex and understanding, hugs and apologies, the clouds parted and we emerged to find ourselves closer, happier, stronger, and more inextricably in love than ever before.

Lockdown was a refining process for our relationship, and I'm now surer than ever that we are a team set to tackle anything life might throw at us next. He has been my lifeboat in lockdown, and I have been his.

111

It's been 111 days since we moved in together. 111 days of spending it with you. 111 days of inside jokes and shared moments that gave me joy like I've experienced with none other. 111 dinners and 111 breakfasts. 111 days of shared emotions and conversations. 111 evenings of Netflix. 111 days of growing affection. 111 evenings by your side. 111 mornings waking up by your side. And in the end, it only took 1 day for it all to disappear.

TOUCHING

I've never liked the idea of anyone touching me; even my mum trying to give me a hug makes me feel uncomfortable. I've never hugged my closest friends. I hate the idea of somebody sleeping next to me.

And then I met my boyfriend. All I want is to be close to him. His hand on my leg when he's driving, his breath on the back of my neck when I'm sleeping, everything. I can't explain why or how but somehow, he's managed to turn something I used to actively avoid into my love language. It was a change I didn't realize I needed in my life and one I'm so grateful for.

ROMANCE ISN'T DEAD

We celebrated Valentine's Day together, yesterday. He got me a kitchen knife. He said roses were too obvious.

Nothing says I love you like an object you can stab them with, I guess?

Now to casually hint for next year that flowers are a better romantic gift than a kitchen utensil...

LOST

I miss the man I used to know. Where did he go?

TASTE OF THE DIVORCED DAD LIFE

At the end of last year, I got into a new job in a city four hours' drive from home. My wife of more than twenty years and I intended to relocate, but we decided that we should avoid disrupting our sons' school year. So, the plan was for me to work there and come back over weekends, until we would all move together eight months later. I got a taste of the divorced dad life and did not like it one bit.

When lockdown happened, my workplace was among the first to send its people home – and home, to me, could be my actual family home. Really, the pandemic got me out of my uncomfortable living situation. My partner, who is a businesswoman-from-home, and I got to experience living together all the time without exception nor workdays. It turned out to be really good. I have been in the process of learning to live with performance anxiety as a husband and lover, and the new sustained proximity forced me into growing further. I learnt to expose my fragility and vulnerability, to express my needs clearly, and to accept the generosity of my partner, who listened to these needs and made room for them. I began to deeply appreciate simple gestures; simple touches, a surprise hug, a teasing rub of the shoulder, a touch of an arm, or hand on a back – these became like tasting exquisite yet familiar wine. I learned to slow down, not do anything and just hang out; sometimes conversing, sometimes just being with her in silence and daydreaming, sometimes just sitting beside each other as we were respectively immersed in our own reading or drawing or crafting or watching TV.

My wife's libido has ups and downs, a phenomenon that I have always felt responsible for – an error, yet one I was convinced of time after time. Lockdown brought her into a down. When the pendulum started to swing back, so to speak, so did we. The sex we have is a mirror to that which we did not have. It is deliberate, desired, present, passionate. It is incandescent.

I have been in love for a long time, and I am more so today.

HE FELL IN LOVE

I fell in love. We were discussing my moving to his city, how we would decorate our own place, what our wedding would be like, our future. Then, one day, I started to struggle to get hold of him. He messaged sporadically. I finally told him we needed to talk. We talked, he reassured me we were okay, he still wanted to be together. The last thing he ever said to me was, 'I'll call you back in a bit.'

He fell in love.

It just wasn't with me.

40 YEARS: UPDATE

It is almost a year to the day since he asked for a divorce. A month later, he told me he had made the biggest mistake of his life – that he still loved me and wanted me back. I said no and walked away. But we had been through so much together over the years, there had been so much love between us. I thought that if there was even the slightest chance we could salvage our marriage, then I should say yes when we met again the following week. The provision being that we would attend relationship counselling together and that he would find a therapist.

In retrospect, and as I realized during our counselling sessions, he was in crisis. His life had shrunk. He could not follow many of his interests and his consultancy work had tailed off. He admitted that he did not have the emotional resources to cope with the sadness he was feeling, and he decided I was the cause. I take responsibility for what happened too. Looking back, I can see that we stopped talking properly, we stopped listening to each other, we didn't plan things to do together. We made assumptions about each other. He is a quiet man, and I mistook his increasing silence for normal behaviour. A few months later, when I asked him how he thought our relationship was going, he had decided that divorce was the only option.

After six months apart, we are now living together again. Being kind and careful, and trying to understand our differences rather than becoming frustrated with them. We are rediscovering spontaneity and realising we can still, after forty years, have fun together. However, I won't deny how badly my confidence and self-belief have been affected. But when I was telling a friend how I could never feel the same about my husband, or my marriage, she said incredulously, 'Why on earth would you want to?'. And she's right. There's no going back to the old ways now. Next year ask me how we are, and I hope I can tell you we are still together.

THE ULTIMATE

He told me that he wants a baby next year or he'll leave me.

Relationships are about compromise; but I can't do that to me, or our unborn child.

I love him so much it physically hurts. But I love me more.

Puppy pending...

BREAK-UPS

Nothing lasts forever. Things change. People grow apart. Some people aren't meant to be permanent residents in our lives. All endings are new beginnings. There are so many clichés about break-ups.

The reality is most break-ups are painful and confusing – even if you're the one instigating it. It's normal to feel a mixture of regret, hope, sadness, loss, loneliness, excitement, fear, guilt and shame. Break-ups are raw; like peeling off a scab to get to silky skin. Sometimes you're going to bleed. Sometimes it's going to leave a scar.

Break-ups are a form of grief, and there are many stages to go through in their aftermath – hurt, anger, bargaining, acceptance. Like a death, a break-up can be sudden or it can be the final step in a long and slow demise. Both are painful.

Relationships should always be a choice. If you are the instigator, the decision to break up is often agonising – the worry of the impact on the other, as well as yourself. The anxiety of other people's reactions. The fear that your future self will regret it. If you are the one being broken up with, feelings of abandonment and rejection are often experienced, which can trigger insecurities and open wounds that pre-date the relationship and run deep.

The stories in this chapter take us through the emotional journey of breaking up: from anger, pain and loneliness, to excitement, hope and growth. They bravely admit the moments of loss of grace; the feeling of hopelessness, the awkwardness, pride, anger and passive-aggressiveness of the first post break-up meet-up. They reveal the relief of extricating yourself from a relationship you didn't want to be in, the darkness of feeling abandoned, the counting of days of loss. Others share the expansiveness of new beginnings, the transformative energy of this time, and remind us that eventually, very often the change we undergo in the recalibration of the self after a break-up is often one that we wouldn't undo given the choice.

Break-ups are a form of liberation, even if you may not have wanted that liberation. When you are uncoupled, there is a return to the self – but it is a new self.

It is in this new self – within the regret, hope, sadness, loss, loneliness, excitement, fear, guilt and shame – that raw, silky skin emerges.

BECAUSE

I broke up with my boyfriend. Because I needed to work on me.

Because I love the other guy.

A SINGLE THING

I broke up with my boyfriend. It was a long time coming and we had been on a break in the weeks prior. I had been running from him subconsciously for years and looking for big and dramatic reasons to end things. Reasons like new opportunities in other countries, rent being too high in the city I was living in. Reasons that weren't simply: I'm not interested any more and I don't know that I ever was to the extent you're supposed to be. I knew he couldn't handle that and that he would take it personally – he would try to pinpoint it to a single thing he did or a flaw he thought he had.

We were on a break when I moved back to my home city, and I called it. I ended it. I'm ridiculously happy with this decision. I always was happier single, and I feel like myself again. He wasn't a controlling guy, it's just I guess I'm not at a place yet where I can feel like myself while being in a relationship. I need total commitment to myself for that, apparently.

PENIS

'I don't want this life,' said the guy who broke up with me twice. He told me that recent life events made him realize that he wanted to be around people he 'loves'. That means his friends, his former female boss and (maybe) his mother. It did not include me.

I hope his penis falls off.

365

It's been nearly 365 wake-ups without you, 365 sun-downs without you, 365 bowls of cereal without you, 365 twenty-four hours and I still cannot bring myself to be without you.

THE BREAK-UP

I still haven't really worked out how to put it: that my boyfriend and I broke up mutually; that I broke up with him; that he broke up with me. It's complicated when someone gives you an ultimatum and then is too cowardly to admit that their wrongdoing is what caused the slow, painful demise of a relationship.

We ended on terms that were this: I finally decided that I deserve to be happy. Staying with him would make me unhappy, ending things would make me unhappy, but at least only one of those would be temporary (I'd hoped).

The loneliness and fear I felt for the next few months were very real and raw. Mourning the end of a relationship is like the death of a best friend. I had so many ironic hopes and thoughts of getting back together, and while it was hard to hear aloud, hearing him say that after years of loving me – loving each other, the promises, the plans – he didn't think we would be together again. It was what I needed to get some closure and push on with my life.

It's lonely to have your heart broken, but I know there are better things for me coming. I have to get up and find them on my own.

9½ WEEKS

Me: I deserve better than how you treated me. If your daughter told you about a man who had acted the way you have, you'd have told her she deserves the world and to get rid of him.

The One: You're right. I am sorry. It was never my intention to hurt you or pick you up and put you down. I am not proud. Your expectations are not wrong and you should expect a lot more than I have given or shown. I really am sorry, it was never my intention to mess you around.

Me: Then why did you?

The One: I really didn't do it on purpose.

Me: You had to know what you were doing, things don't just change overnight. You didn't even have the courtesy to pick up the phone to tell me. Or even text me.

The One: Like I say, I'm sorry. I will call you when I have the chance to talk properly.

That was 9-and-a-half weeks ago. I'm still waiting for him to call.

SNAKE

The snake plant died the other day, the one that I got us both.

I wanted its wilting leaves to symbolise me getting over you,

But you're all I think about still.

Now I have no plant,

And no you.

THE BIG EX

On my birthday, my ex-boyfriend died. The original ex, the big ex, the four-and-a-half years together ex. He was twenty-three. I panicked and went to live with my boyfriend.

As I was grieving and falling apart, he tried to help me, but soon grew bored of my sorrow and we grew apart quickly. In June, we split up and I moved back in on my own. I'm more in love with myself than I've ever been, and never had more love to spare for my family and friends.

Losing an old love and a recent one instilled more love in myself than ever. It's the biggest love story of my life so far.

FUCK YOU, PAUL

The man I had been happily seeing for ten months began working 'crazy hours'. He's a doctor in a hospital so his work is important. *What a noble cause*, I thought.

I wanted to help him and offered support, space, baked goods and entertainment. But he was so busy, I suddenly stopped hearing from him for almost a month.

He is a recovering alcoholic, so I became convinced that he had started drinking again and was ashamed to tell me. I spent two weeks reading everything I could about how to support someone who might have had a relapse.

Finally, one Saturday afternoon, he called. Anticipating the worst, I had prepared a relapse-support speech in front of me. He was making chicken soup, and broke up with me while I could hear the chopping in the background. Apparently, the relationship wasn't going the way he had envisaged.

I very quickly found out the real reason was due to a petite blonde he'd been talking to for some weeks and that he was quite simply a liar and a coward. I find it profoundly sad that I didn't realize that the last time I saw him would be the last. Fortunately, time on my own has made me realize how grateful I am for me and how much more I deserve.

Fuck you, Paul.

THE BREAK-UP: UPDATE

I saw you for the first time in eight months. I was waiting for my coffee order at a café when I heard that distinctive, booming voice ordering your usual at the counter. I certainly wasn't planning to abandon my Americano for your sake (there's my spite), so I braced myself.

You: Hey.
Me: Hi.
You: It's been a while.

(The last time I saw you we were both sobbing in my car, so yeah, it's been a fucking minute.)

Me: Yeah, it has. I thought that was you. Could always
    hear your voice from a mile away.

I spoke with an ever-so-slightly passive aggressiveness to my voice. I turned my attention away to our mutual friend you had met for coffee. The three of us used to be close. I felt your eyes on me but didn't give you the option to make eye contact again. I made my pleasantries and left you to it. You've pretended for so long that I don't exist that it was really the least I could do.

Part of me is waiting for you to shoot your shot and contact me. Reach out. Make amends. Most of me knows that your arrogance and pride will mean that you will never do. Makes closure a difficult thing to achieve.

FFWB

I fell in love for the first time about a year ago. It was fast, intense, beautiful, and really, really tough. So after nine months when he broke up with me, I was left, well, broken.

Yet the past four months since, I have grown in ways I could not have imagined. I have multiple female friends with benefits, and we have incredibly healthy communication, honesty, and openness. It has been liberating, empowering, and most of all, very, very hot.

So, as wonderful as our time together was, I wouldn't choose being with him now for the world.

EX IN NEXT

I love you because you inspired me to learn French, encouraged me to try yoga and introduced me to anal sex.

I hate you because you chickened out of introducing me to your dad, compared me to Korean models on Instagram and thought it was 'funny' to see how I'd react by ignoring my Facebook friend request. Oh, and pressured me into having unprotected sex with you (thanks for the chlamydia, by the way).

I'm now dating someone who asked me to be their girlfriend on our second date, introduced me to their close family and friends within the first three months of dating, and video calls me every day. (And encourages me to go for whatever form of contraception that is good for my body.)

Breaking up with you was hard but was also the best decision I ever made. I deleted more than 10,000 WhatsApp messages from you yesterday. Madison Beer's song epitomises you because you're toxic and I don't even have to try to find the G-O-O-D in goodbye.

HOW I REALLY FELT

I am a nurse, you were 'The Doctor,' but I knew you were never going to be just my friend. Nothing has brought me greater pain last year than the devastation of heartbreak.

For a year, we built a foundation. It was nothing more at the start. Just friends. You had a girlfriend. And I was busy completing Hinge.

Then you split up with her. Said it had been 'over for a while.'

Friendly messages turned into light touching and tactile, subtle moves. We would eat our free meals and laugh while the chaos of the hospital was erupting in the background. A few months later we started to be 'FWB'.

I told myself, I didn't feel a thing. I believed it for a while. And I was the 'cool and funny' girl who didn't get attached, you thought. You know, the one we all pretend to be when we are lying to ourselves.

I justified every red flag you waved in my face. I had never felt so insecure yet so confident at the same time around anyone but you. *What did I do right to be so lucky?*, I thought.

We spent the weekend of my birthday together. You cooked me my favourite meal, and had bought me a present. We had the best sex, the most fun and you made everything else feel so insignificant. It was the best weekend of my life.

One day, without warning, I could feel you slipping away. I still don't know why. But I just knew I wasn't at the front of your mind anymore.

When you finally said you were ready to date and find someone, I thought this was my window to be honest about my feelings. You said you didn't feel the same.

I was a 'great friend and excellent fuck', apparently. Not good enough to be with though, and I felt like my heart had been stabbed.

I was so lost. For a long time, dark and intrusive thoughts regularly infiltrated my mind. *I am nothing. Unskilled and unintelligent.*

Time allowed for friendship. But I will never be comfortable with being just your friend. You still tell me about some girls you've dated and ask for advice. I pretend to be the 'cool girl'. I'm not cool.

You will never know I cried on my way home from every Hinge date because they weren't you, which I'm sure has an impact on my Uber rating. I never told you how much you broke my heart, for the risk of being vulnerable and feeding your ego. Sometimes, I wonder if it would have made a difference.

I have to convince myself every day that you're not my person. It's been almost a year since we first started sleeping together. I would never trade what I felt when we were together, even if it was brief. And now, I am the best version of myself. But of all the loves I thought I have had, there has never been one more passionate, painful and as true as you.

But don't worry, my friend. I would never give you the satisfaction of knowing how I really felt.

WHAT I'VE TRIED: THE BREAK-UP EDITION

I met someone. Someone kind, who brought me so much joy. Who made me feel calm and loved, and helped me realize my self-worth, and I fell in love. But he moved abroad, and the logistics became impossible. He called things off and I felt the full force of heartbreak.

In the aftermath of the break-up, my friends and family propped me up:

They texted and called
They met for endless coffees
They allowed me to exist in their homes so that I wasn't
    alone with my thoughts
They partook in hours of break-up analysis
They always found time to check how I was doing
They sat while I cried and allowed me to grieve without
    judgement
They threw surprise parties and took me on holiday
My mum cuddled and consoled in a way only mums can
They distracted me and teased me; one time they even
    did my laundry
They turned blind eyes when I couldn't concentrate at
    work
They bought friendship bracelets and ridiculed my
    rebounds
They wrote cards and sent little messages to cheer
    me up
They opened up about lost love in their own lives
They gave advice and perspective
They made me smile
They made me laugh
They brought me joy (even when I was still really, really
    quite sad)

They allowed me to remember that I don't need a
romantic partner to be whole and happy and valuable.

I have never felt more loved than in the midst of my
heartbreak. This is not a story about heartbreak, it's a
love story. A love story I feel so lucky and grateful to be a
part of.

NOT AN OPTION

I couldn't settle. You made no effort and treated me like
an option. We're not doing that again this year. I know
my worth. Your loss.

THE ACHE

My boyfriend of nearly seven years broke up with
me, completely out of the blue. The reason? Because
somewhere along the line, during the past year, he'd
fallen out of love with me. He'd wanted to keep this to
himself until he was ready to make a decision about his
future. Only this was our future, *my* future too.

He didn't think my small voice or feelings mattered
enough to tell me when things began to change. He'd
been pretending every time he said 'I love you', or
spoke about our future. It felt like a hole had been
ripped open in me. It had only ever been him. Without
sounding too much like that quote from *Friends*, he
really was the person I used to think would never, ever
hurt me.

Every happy memory was now filled with questioning. I felt as though overnight he'd changed completely and taken our memories with him. Less than three months later, he'd moved on with someone from work. I was still finishing the paperwork for the flat we had shared. I took my time, ached with the sadness of the break-up, and tried to move forwards.

Six months on, pretending that I was fine seemed to feel less contrived. Slowly, I started to feel more like me. I dipped my toe back into dating. I have been seeing someone now for three months but, in honesty, I feel as though I'm no better than my ex was. False appearances, playing a part. He's a good man and I want to be open enough to feel it all again. But quietly, I feel as though my heart has gone cold and I can't thaw it out.

I read the stories of people falling so innocently and wholeheartedly for each other and it makes my heart ache a little that I feel so disconnected from this kind of love. I'm hardened to it. Maybe it's too overwhelming to hope for that, maybe we're all pretending that we're fine.

ALMOST

It's been almost four months since we last spoke.

It's been almost four months since you whispered that you'd wait for me, that no one knows us like we do, that we could have the happily ever after.

It's also the same almost-four months since you paraded your new 'In a relationship with...' status all over social media.

And in those four months, there has been guilt and longing and tarot readings and countless what-ifs.

Three months of anger and the feeling of betrayal and not being able to say your name.

Two months of realisations, being thankful for our time, trying to wish you the best.

And in this last month, it was late in the evening and my head was tired, I typed your name into the search box from memory to find you both standing there, arms around her waist, grinning like a Cheshire cat.

You looked good, and I (almost) felt nothing.

ON THE RUN

I find it somewhat therapeutic to read these stories. To know that it's not just me who got taken in a whirlwind romance, to experience the hurt of the drop. Five months after finding love... I'm here, sitting in a puddle of tears and trying to figure out where it went wrong.

The more I read, the more I realize that so many others struggle with meeting the right person. It's like there are so many factors that have to collide and slot together in a single moment. Unfortunately, a joint love for running, church, or adventure, just won't cut it.

I can't believe what a zombie I've become. I don't think I've ever experienced this kind of grief before. It's made worse with autumn's arrival. I'm not ready to say goodbye to summer or to our time together. I feel like the change in seasons is one of my favourite times normally, but I'm not ready to move on to the next chapter. I'm not ready to let go of the memories or see the days turn short; the mornings and afternoons, dark.

I feel so deeply saddened walking anywhere. I feel like we made so many memories; exploring life and love together. Everywhere I go seems to be covered in a thick layer of silted memories I find myself wading through. I can't walk anywhere now without grieving the loss of that friendship.

It feels cathartic to write about it though. A bit dramatic, but mainly cathartic. To share those memories with a world of people who will never personally know me or my pain, but who I know will understand the feelings. Because I see it – loss happens – Every. Damn. Day. How people don't walk around with gaping holes, I don't understand. Maybe, they do?

I remember that time we spent talking together in the hammock until midnight in the middle of the week, in the fields south of the river. All the times we ran along the river. Our first half-marathon, completed together. When we stood at the foot of the bell tower and held hands for the first time. That time when you carried me across the soccer fields late at night in your arms after mucking around together on one of our late-night walks – just because. We couldn't get out of the field, so we had to climb the fence. You would always walk me home, even though you lived 40 minutes away. Made my heart melt a little.

All those times we sat by the river watching the sunsets and eating. That day we took off work, silly and spontaneous, and rode up to Wimbledon Common to spend a day together. We didn't get home till late, and I had to wrap that stupid cut from my bike in plastic because that's all we had. I taught you two-handed 500 and we ate grapes for days. The cut on my leg healed but left a big purple scar. I think I always looked at it and didn't want it to go because it reminded me of that day together and I remembered it with fondness. So much fondness. Now I find myself searching for ways to try to make it go away.

Those times we would watch storms roll in and were fascinated with their dramatic arrivals. No matter where we were – if we were at home, working, or out, – there would always be some kind of exchange via text to announce the weather change. I was always excited about it, and I feel like you were too. Maybe you were excited because I was.

That time you walked me back to the Santander bikes near your house. You'd given me your credit card, so I could take a bike home, as we had ridden home on them the night before. We'd ridden home as fast as we could so we could spend all the time together. We had both made the decision not to give ourselves away until marriage, so we kissed and talked for hours, and then you went and slept in the spare room. You were always so respectful and careful of that.

That next morning, we stood on the corner of the road and hugged... You talked about waiting for marriage and how it would be good. I laughed and I said, 'It might not be you know, but we will see.' You smiled and said reassuringly, 'I know it will be good, because we had a taste of what it could be like.' I remember feeling gooey in my tummy and appreciating we could talk about it and look forward to something like that. We talked quietly about the possibility of marriage. I don't feel like it was just me. It was mutual. Did that frighten you, deep down? Scare you?

So many memories and moments cycle through in my mind. I'm torn between trying to let them go and move on; trying to understand where we went wrong; and holding on to them so I will never forget this time together. I don't fully understand the why, but somewhere along the line, you cut me out. You said it wasn't anything I did, you just fell out of feelings for me. I never got to tell you I loved you.

There are some days, like today, that I can only summon up in a few words: I miss you so unbelievably much. Even more so, I miss me before you. Sometimes, it feels like I will never heal or ever get better. I'm just going to have to let time take its course, and learn to love me again, after you.

INTO THE UNKNOWN

I broke up with someone whom I was with for slightly less than a decade. We'd been together since university and had gone through ups and downs to try to make long distance work. We amicably decided to go separate ways at the end of our 'make-or-break' year.

It was a big leap of faith, a plunge into the unknown for love. I felt a sigh of relief when we finally came to this decision, it felt like years of heartache and promises that never came to realisation finally went to rest. From here, what next?

THE COOL GIRL

This is not a love story. This is a break-up story.

I'd been single for over nine months, following a very messy break-up with my university boyfriend. We'd tried to rekindle the love we once felt at twenty-two. Inevitably, it wasn't the same at twenty-seven, even with the promise of a ring.

When I downloaded Tinder, I didn't think much of it. I misspent an afternoon chatting to a random. Maybe a bit of sexting. At the very least, it was a way to pass the time while my housemate was away.

When I saw N's profile, I was thought he was cute but nothing more. We matched and did the standard pleasantries, 'How are you?', 'Where do you work?', etc.

It took about four days until I gave him my number. It was a Saturday. I was in the middle of moving my desk up a spiral staircase of our pub-turned-maisonette flat, when he messaged me saying 'Hey, do you mind if I call you?'.

It was so polite, so innocent, that I couldn't help but say yes. A phone call was old-fashioned. It played to romantic notions, the ones in which I still dreamed of a *The Notebook*-style romance with a Ryan Gosling-esque figure. We chatted for an hour, possibly longer. My mouth ached from smiling and I was sad when he finally hung up.

Over the coming days, we talked constantly. We fell into each other's worlds. I learnt about his upbringing in the heart of London, how his mum worked in one of the museums, and his love of travelling. I told him about my love of weird facts, my boring job in The City and my ex. Everything was intense, but wonderfully so. It felt like the beginning of something more, something bigger. I wanted it to be. I hadn't felt the pangs of love like this in years.

It was the little intimacies that I cherished most. The photographs, the mundanity of work. We'd even say good morning and good night. For a very lonely young woman, N became everything.

We FaceTimed. I felt nervous and joked about a lot. Drinks were poured on either ends of the call and then he asked 'How would you feel if I came over?'.

It felt like an eternity him getting here. I wanted to pace around the room, I was so nervous. What if he changed his mind? But when he got to my front door, I rushed into his arms. I stood there in the doorway kissing him, not caring that it was the middle of the night or that I was in my underwear. My world became a bit less lonely.

He stayed the night, and in the morning we showered together and exchanged lazy kisses over cereal on Easter Monday. It didn't feel like a one-night stand, it felt like more. I hoped it wasn't a one-night stand. He left and I couldn't wipe the smile off my face. I'd loved every second of being with N. He had this infectious smile and bright eyes. Just being near him felt like sunshine.

A week later, we were arranging our next meeting when he said, 'I think we need to slow this down. It felt different after we had sex, right?' It was a complete 180 from the day before. I was floored. I couldn't bear him knowing that I'd fallen for him completely. I wanted to be the cool girl. The one that he could see himself with. If only he could let me in.

'No, things haven't changed. Let's keep going,' I replied. From that point on, things felt strained. Maybe he pulled away or maybe my brain felt like he was pulling away. Either way a week later, the discussion cropped up again. I was heartbroken.

This was what I'd been trying to avoid. I had a horrendous habit of going for emotionally unavailable guys. It was the thing that put me off one-night stands; I'd always want to see the person again and they weren't bothered. I wanted so desperately to be loved and couldn't go through the rejection regularly like that, so I stopped. I'd go at least half a year, on a regular basis, without sleeping with anyone. And here I was in the exact scenario I'd wanted to avoid.

It had felt different this time, though. There was a connection, wasn't there? N seemed to agree so. He just didn't want a girlfriend right now. We agreed to remain friends and leave it at that. The one person I looked forward to speaking to, more than anyone else in the world, didn't want to be near me.

Days later, he texted me. Maybe he'd changed his mind, so I texted back. It was just nerves, a blip.

But this time. This time. It would be better. And so began a game of push-pull with my heart.

We'd text, get close, and then he'd pull away. I'd cry, vow to be stronger and then melt when he texted. I lost count of how many tears I shed. I sobbed at my desk, alone at work. I sobbed uncontrollably in the evenings, too. And one very notable moment, when I sobbed taking out the bins, I forgot my keys and had to pay a locksmith £500 to be let back in. I never told N this. I still wanted to be cool girl.

It was around this time, after endless research and Googling, that I decided to try a different approach. If he texted me again, I *was* going to be cool girl. I would be unfazed. I'd be brave. I'd try being a friend with benefits. What did I have to lose? We'd have amazing, world-changing sex and either he would fall for me or I would lose interest. Nothing could go wrong. I'd be like those strong, sex-positive women you see on TV, who played men at their own games. What could go wrong?

When he texted me on my birthday, I was elated. This was it. I went for it, despite the warning from my housemate. N and I agreed to meet two days later. I walked to meet him in a summer dress, the May sun hitting my skin. As soon as he saw me, I was in his arms. It was as if nothing had changed between then and now. The world slowed as we walked together, chatting about everything and nothing. He bought me gelato. As we sat together, eating ice cream, it felt real. As if none of the drama that had gone before had happened. This is what it could be like, me and him.

We made out for the majority of the day – I couldn't not touch him. I stripped off to my new bikini as we settled in the park. He just knew how to make me feel confident and wanted. I even suggested taking a ride to an empty part of town in his car. A session in the newly deserted financial district in broad daylight. This was *meant to be*. This was the sense of rebellion I'd sought all these years. We held hands as he drove and I thought triumphantly, I could do this. I could be less emotionally invested in sex.

The lie to myself didn't last long, as days later he pulled away. I lied to him and said I'd met someone else, so we should leave it. It wasn't such a lie, I had tried to talk to others before he came back. I went home to Cornwall a wreck. Even during this time, he reached out. I lied and said I'd chat with him when I was back in London.

Weeks went by and he messaged again, 'How are you?'. I lied and said 'good' even though the thought of him made my stomach churn. He asked if I was still seeing 'that person'.

'It didn't work out.'

'Why?'

I couldn't go through it again. I wanted to keep away, but I couldn't.

'You.' I said.

I broke. Over the coming days, we chatted like old times, but I felt uneasy. After a day at the beach with the girls acting as a counsel of war, I had to ask him.

'Why now?'

'Because I want to see you?'

'But why now?'

'Well I'm going away for a month and I want to see you.'

And there it was, I was convenient.

I railed and ragged. 'Yes, but why me?'

'Because I like you. I'm fussy and we have this great connection. It's just different, isn't it? I just can't have a girlfriend right now, I'm leaving London in six months to live in Denmark. If I thought I was staying, I'd date you in a heartbeat – you know that, right?'

I was so frustrated, I couldn't tell whether he was feeding me what I wanted or being honest. I asked to call but he said he was busy, but could we still meet. This had to end. I couldn't give anymore of myself. I cried in the arms of my best friend as I agreed to meet after work the next day. This was it.

We agreed on a pub after work. I'd barely eaten all day. I looked exhausted to the point where I'd had to turn off my webcam for the work Zoom calls. He was running late, so I panicked even more. If the toilets had been near, I would have hurled. When he arrived, he could tell something was up. I shook on the bar stool, as the cool girl exterior broke. He bought me an orange juice, but we promptly left after that.

Weeks of emotions cascaded over, I broke down outside the pub. This would be the last time I ever saw him, and my heart was breaking. He walked me to the tube and there we stayed for an hour. I told him that he needed to leave me alone as I'd fallen for him, and I couldn't bare that he didn't feel the same.

He shifted uneasily but agreed. 'I never wanted to hurt you. I care about you, but I should have been honest about dating you, it only hurt you more. I'm sorry. It wasn't about you, I just haven't been emotionally available for a really long time. Especially, now I'm moving. I put in for the transfer at work and I...'

I simply said, 'I just need to be away from you.' For the first time, he looked hurt. 'I think I need to block you'.

'I understand, but I won't block you. You don't deserve that.'

We talked a little more, but it was grey and overcast. I shivered and he ordered me a taxi.

'You sure you don't want to come back to mine?' Half joking, half serious. We still wanted each other even in this moment.

'We know where that would lead.' I said, sobbing and simultaneously, half smiling.

I handed him his jacket as I walked towards the Uber. We hugged and his hand went into my hair as we said goodbye. I can still feel where he placed it, even now.

'Goodbye then.'

'I'll see you around,' he said. And that was that. I got in the cab and lost it completely, driving away as he entered the tube station.

It's been two months since then, and there hasn't been a day I haven't thought of him. I told you this wasn't a love story.

I wasn't able to block him in the end, much to the annoyance of my housemate. He still lingers in my Instagram stories, although I unfollowed him. I constantly want to see him, to reach out. But the truth is, I don't know whether it would make any real difference. I'll never know whether he liked me, like that. Wasn't it just bad timing? Or was the whole thing built-up lust?

I wish I could say that I've been able to date since, that it doesn't hurt every time I see your name, or that I don't look at your Instagram just to see your face. But none of those are true. I still look for answers as to why you couldn't let me in. Did I look too much like your ex? Am I too sensitive? Did I invest too much too soon? Was it just not meant to be?

All I know is this, I will still go into love headstrong. I'll be hurt again, but if I don't act on the feeling then I will always miss my opportunity. Maybe that is the lesson: go for it and live to your fullest because you never know when it might be over. The memories I have made because of you will last me a lifetime, even if you forgot my name within a week.

But for now, I'm still hoping that our time will come. One day. Until then, this has been a break-up story.

NEW BEGINNINGS

My decree absolute finally came through at the start of this year. My husband of twenty years was a magnet for women. He had two serious affairs. The first with a work colleague, for which I forgave him, and we vowed to make things work for our two amazing boys. The second with an ex from uni, which lasted almost nine years. She thought she was building a life with him. He wasn't. She pressured for commitment. Once again, he begged me to forgive him and for us to stay together. I finally walked away. My heart, my self-confidence, my entire world shattered. The divorce process was long and horrible. I thought I would never be able to love, trust or be happy again.

And then friends introduced me to a smart and wonderful man who made me laugh. Slowly our friendship grew into something more. I asked him to move in with me, my sons and our two dogs. I knew that it was a risk, but life is too short to live in fear and regret.

Moving in together made us and me stronger. He helped me to heal – supporting my work, encouraging me to complete my PhD, helping my sons to move forward. Most of all, enabling me to rediscover the amazing woman I had forgotten was inside me. Perhaps the greatest evidence of how far I have come is the fact that I no longer feel anger towards my ex or his former lovers. I am genuinely glad to see him happy with someone new and reconnecting with his sons. He always was a great father. I no longer feel the urge to call his ex's number in the middle of the night and scream down the phone. When I see her posting photos of his football club or favourite band in the hope that he will one day return to her, I long to encourage her to learn to let go as I have. A few weeks ago, my smart and wonderful man asked me to marry him and I said yes. We all deserve new beginnings.

HOME

After experiencing the worst possible break-up from the most toxic relationship I've ever been in, I felt so worthless. He had destroyed the confidence that I spent twenty-six years building. He knew what I wanted, and he dangled that future in front of me. I soon realized that it wasn't the man or the relationship I had been mourning, but the future I could have had.

After a few months living alone, I decided to go home and stay with my family for a while. I had no idea that I'd end up reconnecting with a childhood friend... and falling in love with him. It finally feels like I've found a healthy relationship with someone who knows the real me and makes me feel 'worth it'. I think the break-up has brought about some positives, most of all, it brought me home.

GOODBYE MY LOVER

After being with my boyfriend and love of two-and-a-half years, we realized we both wanted different things. I wanted to write this to reassure you it is a positive thing, to grow. As painful as it may be.

I love you still, but we must grow apart now.

You can anonymously submit and share
your own love story at:
www.its-complicated.com
@itscomplicatedstories

WITH LOVE FROM ME

(ACKNOWLEDGEMENTS)

This is a love story to everyone who contributed to
getting this book into being:

To my agent, Imogen Pelham, who is as cool as she is
clever. Thank you for seeing this book through its many
iterations, and for sending the proposals out one last time,
when others might have told me to give up. Negotiating
this book deal days after having your first baby weeks
early (and only casually dropping that into conversation
after first telling me about book offers) is just beyond. You
are a powerhouse.

To my editor, Ellen Simmons, and the whole team at
Pavilion, Alice Kennedy-Owen in design: every second
of working with you on this book has been pure joy. I
couldn't have dreamt of a better (all-woman) team to bring
this into the world. From day one, we have been on the
same page and that page was big and bold and BRAT and
heartfelt and feminist as fuck. Your vision and ambition
were next level. Working with you has been exciting,
energising, enabling and elevating, and is what all creative
collaborations should be like. It has been so much fun.

To Melissa Bennett and everyone at the Greater London Authority and Groundworks London for the London Community Story Grant which supported the writing of this book proposal. In a world that largely conflates value with money, being awarded financial support for creative ideas is not just crucially enabling but validating.

To the UK Friends of the National Museum of Women in the Arts, Washington: for being the coolest arts patron group and my partner organisation so I could receive the grant. Especially Susan Zimny and Anna Burman for gathering all the paperwork with 24 hours-notice and all your continued support. You truly make a difference to women artists.

To my Fine Art tutors at Chelsea College of Art, which is where this project began: to Ben Fitten for always thought-provoking discussions and Katrine Hjelde, who when I expressed doubts about starting Lockdown Love Stories in April 2020 said, but YOU haven't done it yet. And so I did.

To my Creative Writing tutors at the University of East Anglia Masters: Jeanne McNeil, Henry Sutton, Giles Foden. To Andrew Cowan who published a selection of these stories on New Writing in the early days of this project, and Helen Cross who left my writing a million times better than she found it. To Sam Copeland, for all the advice and calls of recommendation – even five years after the UEA Agent/Mentor programme ended.

To Bernardine Evaristo: Thank you for not just teaching me to write but making me believe I could; for not guarding gates but opening them; and for telling us: if you can't get in through the front door, you go round the back.

To Nancy Jo Sales, for the shout outs.

To all the people who used their platforms to amplify Lockdown Love Stories and in doing so helped gather so many of the stories included in this book.

To the administrative team in at University of the Arts, London, who sent the first email out to spread the word and kick started this project on day zero. To Nina and Liezel at ArtGirl Rising who supported my *Lockdown Love Stories Live from My Bed* performances.

To the Royal Parks for not getting too mad at me, and always signing their emails with a kiss.

To my friend, Louisa Rose, for showing a girl who had never posted an Instagram story how to build and run a project through social media (and get a lot of press!).

To the journalists who wrote features: Anna Russell for *The New Yorker*, Jessica Summers for *MailOnline*, Saman Javed at *Independent*, Almara Abgarian and Tanyel Mustava for *Metro*, Georgia Aspinall at *Grazia*, Lisa Smorsarski at *Stylist* and Elle Hunt for *Observer*.

To Lynsey Evans and Katie Piper at ITV, and Charlotte Wright and Jayne McCubbin at *BBC Breakfast.* To Jo Good, Claira Hermet, and Colin McEnroe who invited me on to their radio shows at BBC and NPR. To Pete May at Heart Radio. Mint Velvet for asking me to write about love in lockdown. Matt Warren who included some of the stories in his book, *Are You Thinking Clearly?,* and the many local presses and online publications who covered the project.

To the TFL staff who platformed the stories: Sophie Kyei-Donkoh at Piccadilly Circus, James Willesden @willesdenstaff, Garima Dubey and Glen Sutherland at Morden and Ann Gavahan. Glen: I loved that whatever I asked, (even if we weren't necessarily supposed to) you always made happen. You are a true supporter of the arts.

To Emily Prideaux, Emma Lange and all the team at Derwent London: I still can't believe we put together a public exhibition across thirteen London sites in three weeks, and you didn't blink at me being 39 weeks pregnant. That we blew up 19 stories so big across shop fronts that unknowing submitters spotted their stories as they passed by on London buses. It was huge, and will forever be one of the best things that ever happened in my life.

To JackArts/BuildHollywood and everyone at Procreate Project for putting a love story on a billboard.

And to the followers of the project on Instagram: who were so respectful and supportive of each other's stories, who sent me thank you messages and who slid into my DMs and became like friends: Giulia, Bethany, Gorki, Liv, Beth, Nikki, Andrea, Charlie, Clair, Rose, James, Laura and so many more. To 'Team Chalk' who literally got on their hands and knees to spread the word across the country. To all the strangers I met while chalking. To everyone who showed this project love, it was the ultimate drug.

From the time of this book's conception to its realisation, I have lived every single one of this book's chapters, which besides the obvious included the sudden death of my best friend, Lucie, and the birth of my second child, Romy. Thank you to everyone who reminded me who I was while I walked through this wild, especially my great friend, Tory.

To Tigs and Romy for the love and light, and for forgiving me when I am absorbed in work. I want you to know that you can follow your dreams. Tigs, your chalks were where this all began. Thank you for the hours you accompanied me on walks to chalk in parks through lockdown to gather stories when you were only 3 years old. And for your endless, ingenious ideas – you inspire me.

To my mum for looking after Tigs and Romy so I could do this, and for always having made me feel capable of achieving anything I wanted. And to Aneta, for always stepping in to look after the kids whenever I needed. To my dad and gran, though they are no longer here, for instilling in me a love of the written word and a belief in its power. To my sister, Francesca, who worked at Lockdown Love Stories HQ for six months. All creatives need someone to inject outside energy and work through ideas – and you did that and so much more. (Your pop culture references and sourced images were on point). To Simon for your support, belief and always valuing my creativity. To my brother, Oi-Oi, for how you see me and what you say to me. To my creative writing cohort who always support and encourage. To my friends: Gillian who said, 'When lockdown was announced I knew you'd do something brilliant'; and to Lucie who said it was impressive.

But my biggest thanks of all, without question, is to the story submitters: To every person who trusted me to be the guardian of their truths – in all their raw, sticky, glittering, complex, razor honesty - I felt every word. To gather your burning truths and fire them into the world was a privilege and a joy. Thanks to you, we can better see now.

Thank you.

P.S.
(ABOUT THE AUTHOR)

Philippa Found is an artist, writer and curator based in London. Her short stories have been published by Galley Beggar Press and prize listed for the Bath Short Story Award, The White Review Short Story Prize and the Galley Beggar Press Short Story Prize among others. Her artwork has been exhibited in multi-site exhibitions on the London Underground and across the London High Street, and has featured in *The New Yorker*, *Independent*, *The Mail Online*, *Grazia*, *Stylist*, *Metro*, *BBC Breakfast* and ITV's *Lorraine*.

Between 2006-2012 Philippa was the Director and curator of ROLLO Contemporary Art, London, a commercial gallery unique at the time for specialising in the representation of women artists. She curated exhibitions at the Royal Academy of Arts, London, Selfridges, London and the New Hall Art Collection, Cambridge; and published a three-part non-fiction book, *The Body in Women's Art Now*, which was nominated for the Feminism and Women Studies Book Award, 2011. In 2010 she was invited to be a founding member of the Art and Gender Research board at Centre Pompidou, Paris.

Throughout her career, Philippa has worked to redress the under representation of women in the arts and believes in storytelling as a radical feminist act.

Philippa-found.com

NOTES